Living and Loving the Mystery

Living and Loving the Mystery

Exploring Christian Worship

DUNCAN B. FORRESTER

SAINT ANDREW PRESS
Edinburgh

First published in 2010 by
SAINT ANDREW PRESS
121 George Street
Edinburgh EH2 4YN

ISBN 978 0 7152 0911 0

British Library Cataloguing in Publication Data
A catalogue record for this book is available from the British Library

It is the Publisher's policy to only use papers that are natural and recyclable and that have been manufactured from timber grown in renewable, properly managed forests. All of the manufacturing processes of the papers are expected to conform to the environmental regulations of the country of origin.

Typeset by Waverley Typesetters, Warham, Norfolk
Printed and bound by Bell & Bain Ltd, Glasgow

Contents

Preface

This book is intended to help 'people in the pew' to understand and enjoy worship. It is hoped to encourage them to engage with the mystery of God's love, and in particular to grasp the principles of Christian worship and the structures within which God's people have found that they may best glorify and enjoy their God. It is not easy to produce a simple definition of worship. For me, the best description is still to be found in the answer given to the first question in the Westminster Shorter Catechism (1648): 'Man's chief end is to glorify God and enjoy Him for ever.' In spite of the time-boundedness of the seventeenth-century sexist language, those dozen words sum up both the intimate and the transcendent nature of worship. This speaks of worship both as ascribing to God the glory that properly belongs to God and also as delighting in God's company. It suggests that worship is a central, characteristically human, and virtually universal activity of humankind.

This book does not claim to be a definitive study or a comprehensive history of worship. It aims to help people who worship in church to understand more and to participate more fully. It raises questions and should provoke well-grounded discussion. There are lots of stories and illustrations to 'earth' the discussion; and questions are suggested at the end of each chapter to stimulate debate and further questioning. I hope that church groups of various traditions will find the book accessible and stimulating. Although it is produced in Scotland, it is expected that it will circulate and be used in other lands as well.

My interest in worship was profoundly shaped by eight years as a missionary in southern India, followed by eight years as chaplain and lecturer at the University of Sussex. For some twenty-three years, I taught Christian Worship at Edinburgh University. In all those contexts, students and colleagues have been stimulating and helpful, especially my colleagues in writing *Encounter with God: An Introduction to Christian Worship and Practice* (London: T&T Clark, 3rd edn, 2004), Dr Gian Tellini and the late Dr J. I. H. McDonald. The substance of that book's chapter 6 reappears in Chapters 9 and 10 of this book with the kind permission of Continuum International Publishing Group. Biblical quotations are from the RSV unless otherwise stated.

But my greatest debt is to my wife, Margaret, who is also my minister, and from whose conduct of public and private worship I have learned more than I can say. In the sphere of worship, she combines rigorous criticism with a passion for clarity and beauty of language. She has taught me much of the wonder of loving and living the mystery of God's grace and truth. Her hand may be discerned in a number of places in this book; and I am deeply grateful to her for her encouragement and help in this project.

Duncan B. Forrester
9 June 2010

1

What is Worship?

Worship down the Ages

The historian going back through the ages cannot but be struck by the evidence everywhere that human beings have always worshipped. The oldest archaeological evidence suggests that worship in some form or other occupied a central place in the activity of people from the dawn of history. We cannot find an age or a culture when people disposed of their dead like so much rubbish; always there is some ritual accompaniment to burial or cremation, suggesting not just the awareness of a transcendent order, but also a worshipful attitude towards it. Primitive stone circles, ancient tombs, ruined temples in the jungles, wayside shrines and standing crosses, basilicas in Ravenna, mosques in Cairo, Gothic cathedrals – all remind us of the strange persistence with which people have worshipped all down the ages, and of the importance they allocated to their worshipping. Often, we can know but little of the ordinary life of an ancient people – what they ate and wore, what their homes were like and so forth – yet we have, in contrast, multifarious evidence of their worship. Things to do with worship were made to last, whereas ordinary life has left comparatively scant trace behind.

It is not only the past that is replete with evidence that people have worshipped; the contemporary world is full of shrines, temples, mosques, churches, gospel halls, meeting houses, places where activity relating to the holy – what the German theologian Rudolph Otto spoke of as the *mysterium tremendum et fascinans* – an awesome and fascinating mystery – takes place. The little plain and forbidding corrugated-iron church in a remote glen in the Scottish Highlands, the Pentecostal shop-front church in Harlem, and the glorious Gothic splendours of Chartres Cathedral with its vibrant stained-glass windows are all places of worship.

Is it true that, in the West, at least, society has become secular, worship seems to have less and less of a recognised place, and fewer and fewer seem to take part in any recognisable form of worship? There is force in the argument, let that be admitted; but, although the formal expressions of Christian worship may play a less significant role in most Western societies than once they did, these very societies are not as free from worship as might appear at first sight.

There are, of course, societies in the West where Christian worship continues to hold a central place, as if to mock the sociologists' generalisations about secularisation – Poland and the United States are good examples. And, even in societies where few seem to attend worship frequently, an amazing number of people feel the need to mark the great turning points of life – birth, maturity, marriage, death – with Christian rituals or 'rites of passage', which give meaning to these turning points and allow them to be understood in the context of eternity. This may be residual Christianity, or it may be something more. The conviction that the great moments of celebration, fear, grief and mystery in life can best be marked by Christian worship should not be dismissed as sheer superstition or slavery to tradition. It suggests some continuing relationship to the Christian faith and the worship of the Church which must be taken seriously.

The worship of civil religion is also alive and well. Crowds come to church on Remembrance Sunday who are not seen again in church for another twelvemonth. For decades before the collapse of communism, long queues continued to shuffle past the embalmed body of Lenin in his mausoleum in Moscow's Red Square in a strange ritual of communist civil religion. In communist East Germany, they held Marxist 'confirmations' to try to wean away the young from the Church. And Hitler had a multitude of rituals to confirm and express loyalty to the state and to the evil and perverse ideology of Nazism. Folk religion continues to flourish and to influence not just baptisms and weddings but also, above all, that great modern feast, the harvest festival. And, alongside all this, there is the proliferation of sects that worship or meditate or dance through the streets in ways which seem strange and somewhat disconcerting to the more conventional Christians – the Hare Krishna folk, the Moonies, and the devotees of countless Eastern gurus.

Worship continues in a multitude of forms, some of them bizarre, others but 'vain repetitions' of rituals which seem to have lost their meaning. It is not just the hobby of a few, like squash or model railways: an astonishingly large proportion of humankind takes part in worship with some awareness of its significance, at least from time to time. People seem to be worshippers – you could almost define them as such. That is not to say that everyone worships God, but that everyone at some time worships something.

Worship Today

The Westminster Shorter Catechism suggests rather strongly that worship understood as the cultivation of a proper relationship to God is the central and most important thing in human life. Worship focuses and enriches the whole of life, giving meaning to existence. Humans are made for worship above all other activities. Just to make statements like these in modern secular and fragmented society is to invite ridicule; after all, even 'religious people' are not infrequently embarrassed about the fact that they pray and participate in worship. It seems somewhat anomalous; it doesn't seem to 'fit' in the modern world – or only as a quaint museum-piece, or a furtive and surreptitious activity indulged in by little curious cliques of cranks.

If you look at other contemporary cultures, the situation is far different. A number of years ago, I travelled, wedged tightly in a crowded and sweltering third-class compartment, in a train from Agra to Kanpur in India. After an hour or so, a woman who had been sleeping, squatting under a blanket on the bench opposite, stirred, sat up, elbowed her neighbours until she had cleared about a foot of space on the bench beside her, and opened a tin box. She took from the box a tiny brass image, a religious picture, a little bell, oil, a lamp and a string of beads. She laid these objects on a white cloth, poured oil into the lamp and lit it. For half an hour or more, she performed her *puja*, her worship, ringing the bell with one hand while with the other she swung the little lamp before the image, all the while singing a hauntingly beautiful *bhajan*, a prayer song. When she had finished, she bundled everything away into the tin box and pulled the blanket back over her head, but one could still hear her low whispering and see the little movements as she went over her prayer beads. Nobody, whether sitting, standing or hanging onto that compartment (and there must have been close on fifty people within sight of her – the coach was rather like a swarm of bees) paid any attention to her or her *puja*. It was just part of life; an important part, perhaps, but perfectly natural and not deserving of special attention or comment – save by the Christian from the West sitting opposite, who found his own assumptions and attitudes to worship and its place in life challenged and disturbed!

Or sit in the lounge of a Westernised Hindu businessman's house, chatting while we wait for breakfast. The conversation flows smoothly and naturally, but to the Westerner rather incongruously, from the problems of inflation to the miracles of Sai Baba, who produces coins and watches out of the air; from labour troubles to the forthcoming pilgrimage to Sabarimalai, in which our host intends to join after three weeks of ritual purification; from the political situation to the beneficial effects on businessmen of meditation – and, all the while, incense is drifting into the room and there is a gentle background of tinkling bells and soft singing from next door, where the morning *puja* is beginning. We join in and have a soft running commentary that we may understand. The *puja* finished, we all go through to breakfast. The worship is a natural, central and determinative dimension of the life of the home and family.

Or stand outside a busy suburban station in Chennai (Madras) during the evening rush hour, and watch how many of the businessmen with their suits and rolled umbrellas, and the clerks and the unskilled labourers as they pour out of the station, stop at the little shrine of *Ganesh*, the elephant god, to spend a few minutes in prayer, or circle the shrine three times, or make an offering of flowers, or of rice, or of money. Once again, worship is accepted without embarrassment or self-consciousness as a natural and necessary part of life. How different from the Western tendency to fragment everything and to regard worship as a private hobby of the few, without public relevance, incongruous and curious, in a modern society!

It is, of course, dangerous and misleading to exaggerate the contrast between East and West, and romanticise the Eastern attitude to worship. Not only do a vast number of people in the West take part at least from time to time in some form of worship, but also almost everyone seems to have at least a surrogate for worship, if not 'the real thing'. And everyone who takes part in worship has some awareness that this is an activity which focuses life, allocates priorities, gives meaning and strength, and is the nourishing of a relationship with what is of ultimate importance.

Worship and Relationship

Indeed, the nourishing of a relationship is near to the heart of what Christians and most other religious people understand as worship. The best images of worship are drawn from the field of personal relationships. And, if one really believes that God is impersonal and incapable of relating to men and women in a personal sort of way, worship becomes meaningless or mechanical and is quickly abandoned or allocated a very lowly and insignificant place. Certainly, if we are to understand worship in the light of the Westminster Shorter Catechism as 'glorifying and enjoying God', there is the clear presupposition that God is pleased to relate to people in a personal sort of way.

Etymologically, the English word 'worship' means the recognition and celebration of 'worth', value, goodness and holiness, wherever such qualities are to be found. The archaic language of the 1662 Anglican Prayer Book reminds us of other dimensions of the meaning of worship. In the marriage service, the groom says to the bride: 'With my body I thee worship.' He responds, that is, in the most appropriate way to his beloved: he recognises and celebrates her worth and value to him, her lovableness. And this he does not only in words – the words of lovers are often pretty incoherent! – but also with the body. Love is expressed and strengthened in bodily acts; it is something that involves the whole personality. The kiss, the cuddle, gazing silently into one another's eyes, sexual intercourse – these are just some of the bodily ways in which love shows itself. And lovers, like worshippers (indeed, my argument is that they are very much the same thing), use symbols that are charged with rich meaning: the bunch of flowers, the ring, the gift of perfume and so forth. These are just some of the ways in which partners recognise and celebrate the love and worth of each other. They communicate with one another in verbal, bodily and symbolic ways, and their communication both shows that love is there and deepens and enlarges and strengthens the love between them.

This image of worship reminds us of various things. First of all, worship is a *relationship* between God and people, which must be reflected in the quality of relationship between the worshippers and in their attitudes to their neighbours.

Second, the relationship involved in worship is, like love between partners, a *reciprocal relationship*. It is right and proper that we should emphasise that worship is the recognition and celebration of the glory and worth of God – the 'glorification of God', in the terms of the Shorter Catechism – and that this should have an absolute priority in our understanding of worship as a human activity. But it is also true that, in worship, the worshipper experiences an affirmation of worth and value to God. She or he comes to worship aware of sins, confesses them and experiences the forgiving grace and love of God, the divine confirmation that, despite all, the worshipper is loved with an infinite love and is a person of incalculable value to God.

Worship, then, should be a relationship with God in which we enjoy God. It shows, even in the midst of oppression, poverty and the bleakest of outward circumstances, the delight of keeping company with God, in whom all true joys are to be found. Of course, this applies to the whole of the Christian life; but worship, even if it percolates throughout the whole of life as it should, is still the time set apart specifically for loving attention to God.

In families, time needs to be kept for doing things together, for enjoying one another, for talking, for playing together. Of course, those times together are not the whole of the family relationship, but without them the relationship tends to wither and die. If a husband is never at home, always late at work, or out at the pub, or off fishing with his mates, his relationship with his wife and children is put under strain. Consciously or unconsciously, they are likely to conclude that he no longer likes being with them or enjoys their company; and the love can easily wither. We need, in other words, to make time for God, jealously guarded time, in which we give loving attention to God, that the whole of our lives may be lived consciously as a loving relationship with God. And this demands that times of worship are so arranged that we may indeed enjoy God, celebrating God's love and goodness, communicating honestly, and finishing the time of worship wishing there were more but knowing that the whole of life is worship, and that what has been said and done in the special time of worship must be lived out in daily life.

Worship is enjoying God. In worship, our attention is directed away from ourselves, to God and to our neighbours. We do not 'enjoy ourselves' in worship. Indeed, the very opposite: at the start, we look at ourselves honestly and confess our sins; then, as forgiven sinners, we can cease to be absorbed by self and can open ourselves to God and his glory, and to our neighbours and their needs. C. S. Lewis, in his autobiography *Surprised by Joy*, describes how, as a young man, he was engrossed with his own inner workings. He constantly and morbidly scrutinised his motivations, his attitudes and his feelings as if these were matters of cosmic moment. Conversion drew him out of himself; he became far more open to other people, far more sensitive to their feelings, because he was now open to God. Sin, according to a phrase much used by Augustine and Luther, consists of being *incurvatus in se*, turned in on oneself. C. S. Lewis found an amazing release from this obsession with self when he was given the capacity of enjoying God and consequently his neighbour. And understanding worship as enjoyment of God should save us from the trap of becoming obsessed with the minutiae of liturgy and the details of worship as if these things were important in themselves rather than simply as aids, which should be unobtrusive, to the glorification and enjoyment of God by all God's people.

Questions for Discussion

1. What kinds of Christian worship flourish today?
2. In what ways does worship involve an encounter with God?
3. Why do so many people in Western societies seem to feel no need for worship today?
4. Should we *enjoy* worship?

2

Celebrating Mystery

Mystery

Over 400 years ago, in February 1589, a remarkable series of sermons was preached in the High Kirk of Edinburgh. The preacher was Robert Bruce, one of the outstanding figures in the early days of the Reformed Kirk. The title of the sermons was *The Mystery of the Lord's Supper*, and they show very movingly how important the Lord's Supper was in the life and witness of the Scottish Kirk from the time of the Reformation, and how, from the beginning, the Scots reformers saw religion as celebrating a *mystery*. These sermons have been very influential down the years on generation after generation of Scots Presbyterians – and on others as well.

What do we mean by a 'mystery'? In everyday language, we think of a mystery as a kind of puzzle, a brain-teaser, perhaps something to do with the uncanny, something that sends shivers down our spines. Or a mystery is something we should be able to sort out, unravel, understand. We get irritated and perhaps angry if we can't solve the puzzle. We think we should be able to make mysteries manageable. We should be able to deal with them, to lay them out in words, or translate them into terms we can understand, to control them. In Douglas Adams' *The Hitchhiker's Guide to the Galaxy*, the answer to the mystery of the universe was, famously, 42. We laugh because we know that such a question cannot have so neat an answer. Indeed, the ridiculous answer underlines the seriousness of the question.

The mystery with which we are concerned as Christians is indeed the secret of the universe. It is something we can't control, or get our minds round, or capture in words. It is the mystery of which we read in Paul's Letter to the Ephesians, the mystery of God's purpose, which was concealed for ages and is now made known through the Church.[1] It is the mystery that has been hidden from the learned and wise and is now revealed to the simple. It is the mystery of the universe contained in the commonplace.

Encountering Mystery

We all encounter true mystery from time to time. Think of holding a new-born baby, your own child, in your arms for the first time. You count the little fingers and toes: ten of each. Perfect, each with a tiny nail, and so incredibly small! You look at the little squashed-up nose, and listen to the breath going in and out so purposefully. There's the dome of the head, and the place at the top where the skull has not yet formed and you can see a pulse. And the eyes, taking in a whole new world, or closed in determined sleep. What a mystery that child is. *Your* child – and you know how babies are made, but still it is a mystery, the mystery of new life, the mystery of a new person, precious, wonderful, exciting, mysterious.

Or think of falling in love. You have known each other for some time, perhaps, but then, one day, the two of you fall in love. You don't calculate and plan: 'On the fourth of November we shall fall in love'. It just happens, mysteriously. And the one you love loves you. You are accepted as you are, you are affirmed, you are loved. It's a great and wonderful mystery which leaves you walking on air, excited, thrilled, a little frightened too: can it be true? Can it last? People who are in love know that they are involved in a mystery which is beyond their control or understanding, and which puts them in touch with something that is very real.

Or have you stood at the bedside of someone who is dear to you and has just died? There's the body, so familiar and so loved. But the person has gone. We feel the dreadful wrench of parting. And all our tidy little ideas appear quite inadequate to grapple with this awesome mystery. However we manage to cope with our grief and with the confusing whirlpool of emotions which tosses us about, we believe that we are in touch with a profound, mysterious and inescapable reality.

Experiences such as these put us in touch with profundities we cannot get our minds around. They lie too deep for us to capture them fully in words. In the face of mystery, we do not chatter. We weep, and we wonder, and sometimes we laugh. We encounter mystery in the commonplace, in ordinary simple things – babies are being born, people are falling in love, people are dying all the time. But sometimes we see that these ordinary things are rich with extraordinary meaning. They put us in touch with something that is real and ultimate. It may be painful or delightful, but it is real.

These are mysteries hidden from the wise and prudent, and revealed to babes. Think of a young child's delight at the candles on a birthday cake. Remember the wonder with which a toddler explores its world.

Mystery beyond Words

When we encounter mystery, we are dealing with meaning we cannot easily put into words. Our words are not big enough for the mystery. We need words, but we need more than words if we are to engage with mystery.

Words, words, words: they shriek at us from radio and television; trying to sell us things; tempting words; entrancing words; angry words; charming words. The words of politicians, arguing, cajoling, trying to win votes. The words of preachers, six feet above contradiction. The words of salesmen and advertisers, trying to convince us that we need things. The words of teachers and intellectuals, often bamboozling us. Words used to manipulate us. Words used as weapons.

We are saturated with words. Is it at all surprising that we are pretty sceptical about words? Most of us would happily agree with Eliza Doolittle in *My Fair Lady*, that there are far too many words! When we are in love, we want to show it. When we are in love, we want a response of love – not more words.

Join the Party!

Worship is rather like a party, celebrating a mystery we do not fully understand. The 100th psalm is typical of many passages in the Bible which see worship as something like that:

> All people that on earth do dwell,
> Sing to the Lord with cheerful voice.
> Him serve with mirth, his praise forth tell,
> Come ye before him and rejoice.

Note that we are called to serve him with *mirth*! A good and mirthful party demands meticulous preparation and attention to detail on the part of the organisers. They must give careful attention to the choice, preparation and layout of food and drink; to arrangements of flowers and candles; to lighting and music. They should be careful to invite a good mix of participants; they should ensure that people are introduced to one another; they should arrange the furniture to encourage conversational groupings; and good hosts move people around from time to time to keep an eye open for guests who are lonely or sad, or who just don't fit in. Details such as these are all-important and contribute to the making of a good party in which people enjoy themselves and one another. And it is not only the role of the hosts that matters; guests who wish to enjoy a party will ask themselves questions like these: do I take flowers or a bottle of wine for my hosts? Do I offer to wash up the dishes, or to help hand round food and drink? Do I bother to meet some new people rather than sticking with my old cronies all evening?

Parties, well-arranged parties, parties that people enjoy, are important. When I was a university chaplain, my wife and I discovered how much a good party could do for someone who was disturbed or confused or just plain lonely – but a bad, poorly arranged and cliquish party only made matters worse! And parties are significant for any group of friends, as a way of expressing and cementing and extending their friendship and enjoyment of one another.

If worship is like a party, it is clearly necessary that people who lead worship or participate in worship should know something of what it is all about and be meticulous in their planning and arrangement of worship. The mechanics must be unobtrusive; the arrangements are no more than vehicles to enable the glorification and enjoyment of God. But, when the arrangements are sloppy or inadequate or ill-thought-out, they become obtrusive and detract from the spirit of worship.

Worship and Storytelling

Worship and storytelling are remarkably close to one another. Each Hindu temple has its particular myth or story which slots into the structure of the great tradition of Hinduism. In Israel, the shrine at Bethel had in the story of Jacob's ladder its own foundation myth, relating the shrine and the worship that went on there to the story of Israel. In worship, stories are retold, re-enacted, recalled, meditated upon, and the story of the community of faith is grafted together with the stories of the individual worshippers.

When the kings of the old Anglo-Saxon kingdoms of England were converted to Christianity, they had to look afresh at their personal stories as represented by their genealogies. These traced their ancestors back many generations to the old Norse gods – Thor, Wodin and so on. Rather than renounce their stories, deny their history and assume an entirely new identity, the Anglo-Saxon kings simply extended their genealogies backwards, so that now, as Christians, they traced their ancestry *through* the Norse gods to the patriarchs of the Old Testament and back to Adam! They had grafted their stories into salvation history, and assumed a Christian identity without a total repudiation of the old. In less dramatic and problematic form, people have to relate their personal story to the story of the community – and worship is one of the crucial places where this grafting takes place.

Later, we shall see in greater detail how the Jewish Passover reminds us of another central characteristic of all worship in the historical religions of Judaism, Christianity and Islam: in worship, we find our place in time and understand the present moment by looking back and by looking forward.

Looking Forward

Worship would quickly become maudlin and nostalgic and disabling if it were simply concerned with the past. Worship looks towards the future and encourages hope and expectation, because the God who meets us, the people of God, in the present and dealt with us graciously in the past is also the God who will be with us in the future, when all worship will find its fulfilment and culmination in the immediate presence of God. Worship points forward with confidence, and nourishes people's hope and expectation. Once again, the Passover is an excellent illustration of this.

At times when Jews have been oppressed and persecuted, even in the horrors of the concentration camps, they have celebrated the Passover, not simply as a remembrance of a past deliverance, or as an affirmation that before God they have the status of beloved and free men and women despite the agonies of their outward condition, but also as a way of nourishing their hope for freedom and their expectation that God has some good thing in store for them.

In New Testament times, the Passover season was a time when the revolts against foreign rule were particularly likely because messianic expectations were then at their peak. Worship continues to be the parent of hope.

In most of the Eastern religious traditions, worship is commonly (but not universally) understood as a way of escape from a temporal process, which is itself meaningless, into a timeless realm of spiritual verities. In Judaism, Christianity and Islam, on the other hand, worship is the point at which one can glimpse the significance of history, of the temporal process, as the place where one meets and serves God. In worship understood as the encounter with the God who acts in history, the worshipper is enabled to locate herself or himself in time.

God's Dwelling

A Hindu temple is the abode of a divinity. The priests and other functionaries are attendants and courtiers; the worshippers come individually or in small groups to have *darshan*, audience, of the god or goddess, to meet, to give offerings and to submit petitions. The daily routine and ritual of the temple is closely analogous to that of an old-style royal court. In the early morning, the god or goddess is awoken with music, washed, dressed and offered food. The temple gates are opened to worshippers when the divinity is ready to give audience. Then he or she has the midday meal, and a time of siesta in the heat of the afternoon. Once a year, the god or goddess is borne out of the temple on a great decorated temple car and tours domains, hauled around the streets by hundreds of devotees.

Most temples and shrines of most religions are much like that, although the Jewish temple had no representation of God in its Holy of Holies, and the Jewish faith consistently affirmed that God does not dwell in temples made by hands. But, for all that, the temple was central to Jewish devotion until, after its destruction in AD 70, the synagogue had perforce to take much of the place once occupied by the temple. In such a context, it is easy to understand the surprise and antagonism aroused by the early Christians' claims that they, unlike the Jews and the pagans, had no shrines and altars and, furthermore, that the *community* was the temple of God. God does not live in a building[2] but is present with us, the people of God, who are therefore a living temple, God's temple.[3] Hence the buildings used for worship were meeting places for the community rather than dwelling places for God, and the earliest Christians showed no interest whatsoever in ecclesiastical edifices. They met in houses, or large rooms, or in the open air because they were convinced that the Church was people, not buildings. Some modern hymns capture well the early Church's understanding of itself: they proclaim in song that the Church is not a building, but where the people are, singing and praising and doing acts of service in the name of Jesus.

Worship is, then, the activity of the people of God. It is otherwise called *liturgy*, a Greek word which means the public service or *work* of the people of God. Worship is not something the people of God watch, a kind of stage-show laid on for them as the audience; nor is it something they listen to, like a lecture. Rather, it is something they *do*, and do together. It is the central activity of the Christian fellowship which creates as it expresses: friendship with God and with each other.

Two further points need to be made concerning worship and community. First, worship makes manifest both the belief and the nature of the community of faith. If the worship of a congregation suggests that it is a kind of exclusive club of the like-minded, of people of the same sort who find it easy to get on with one another and happen to 'like that sort of thing', it is radically defective as Christian worship, defective precisely because the Church is a community of all sorts of people, of people who often do not find it easy to get on with one another, but have this one vital thing in common – that they have been called together by God and entrusted with shared responsibilities for witness and service. Christian fellowship is no superficial togetherness, in which people share a smile but don't really know or trust one another enough to share their weakness and need, but is instead a deep, welcoming, honest and supportive community of people who find their deepest encounter with God and with one another in the context of worship. Similarly, if a congregation's worship suggests that it is inward-looking, concerned to preserve its own life at all costs, uninterested in the world around it and indeed an escape-hatch from the ambiguities and tensions of everyday life, its defects as a worshipping Christian community are made obvious. Christian worship is the activity of a community which sees itself as living by grace, existing for the sake of others, open to strangers, and concerned for the world – a community with a mission.

In the second place, in worship the individual not only appropriates a history and enters into a relationship with God but also finds a particular place in the household of faith. The question of identity is resolved in part by the discovery that one belongs within this particular community, stretching far beyond the visible fellowship gathered to worship God to encompass the whole Church down the ages and in every land, the Church on earth and the Church in heaven – the whole *communio sanctorum*, the communion of the saints.

Questions for Discussion

1. What is distinctive in Christian worship?
2. Why does the Bible stress the need to link worship and the doing of justice?
3. 'Serve Him with mirth' – is this possible today? And if so, how?

Notes

1. Ephesians 3:1–13.
2. Acts 7:48–50, 17:24.
3. 1 Corinthians 3:16–17, 6:19; Ephesians 2:21; 2 Corinthians 6:16.

3

In Spirit and in Truth

Who Worship?

Other words are used elsewhere in the Christian churches for worship – the central, defining reality for the people of God. As we saw in the previous chapter, *liturgy* is a Greek term which means 'the work of the people of God'. This reminds us that worship is not simply something that God's people watch passively, as does a cinema audience; nor is it something that goes on invisibly and sometimes inaudibly. It is the central *work*, or activity, of the *whole* people of God. It flows into the rest of life, challenging, encouraging, illuminating, questioning, comforting, disturbing. It is not something that priests or ministers *do*, and the people watch and listen. The people are expected to be active participants, for it is their worship. Priests, ministers, bishops and others who lead worship are simply the *leaders* of the people's worship, and it makes no sense for them to conduct worship alone.

Who worship? The simplest answer to this question is that millions of Christians and people of other faiths around the globe worship in a huge diversity of ways, some of which appear to us to be bizarre, while others are deeply moving even to those who do not share the particular faith that relates to a specific form of worship. Our special concern in this book is with Christian worship, which once again takes a huge variety of forms. But all Christian worship at heart is recognising, celebrating and responding to the supreme worth of God, who loves us with an everlasting love. Christian worship is loving and living the great mystery of God's love for us and for the whole world.

With the exception of the Quakers and other small Christian sects, all Christian traditions have emphasised, often excessively, the role of the minister or priest in worship, sometimes at the expense of the participation of the people, who easily become passive observers and hearers rather than celebrants. The Church of Scotland, for instance, gives the responsibility for the conduct of public worship and the education of the young to the minister, under the discipline of the Presbytery. Nowadays, deacons and readers also lead worship.

The Church of England makes the point even more strongly in declaring that only an episcopally ordained priest may preside over the service. A lay person may preside but only when absolutely necessary.

In the Roman Catholic Church, the Decrees of the Council of Trent in the sixteenth century emphasised with extraordinary strength the exclusive power of the priest:

> The Sacred Scriptures show, and the tradition of the Catholic Church has always taught, that this priesthood was instituted by the same Lord our Saviour, and to the Apostles and their successors in the priesthood was the *power* delivered of consecrating, offering and administrating His Body and Blood, as also of forgiving and retaining sins.

The Second Vatican Council, in a real sense, restored Roman Catholic worship as the liturgy of the people and quietly laid aside many dominant emphases of the past. There were dissidents, of course, who resisted the renewal of worship in the Roman Catholic Church, and in particular the active participation of the people. The most prominent of them was Archbishop Lefebvre. In particular, he scorned the liturgical renewal of that Council, calling the new Mass a Protestant or Democratic Mass. And he urged people to follow the old Mass.

In many Eastern Orthodox churches today, there is a screen adorned with icons of saints which ensures that, when the Holy Mysteries are celebrated, the people can hear what the priest is saying and intoning behind the screen but cannot see what is happening – what the priest is doing. That is too holy for the eyes of 'common Christians'!

Most Christians today, however, would now want to emphasise that worship is the liturgy of the community rather than just of the ordained. The people as a whole, rather than the priest or minister, are the celebrants. The priest is there in a representative capacity. He, or she, represents the whole Church, perhaps even Christ himself, to the local congregation gathered to worship. But this leaves open a variety of interesting questions, some of which we will address later in this book, about the role of the ordained person in the leadership of worship and the life of the community. Meanwhile, it is good to note that, in the early Church, the emphasis was strongly on the presence of Christ in the fellowship, and on the integration of life and worship. The New Testament at no place concerns itself with the question of who presides at the Eucharist, or Great Thanksgiving. The whole community concelebrated with Christ, and there was little interest in who presided. In the early centuries, the role of the ordained in worship was a matter of good order rather than a guarantee of the validity of the worship.

Worship and Justice

We have seen that worship is to be understood as focal moments in our relationship to God and our neighbours. If these two dimensions in worship – the vertical relationship to God and the horizontal relationship to the neighbour – are separated, worship degenerates into a parody of itself. The Old Testament prophets never tired of proclaiming that worship separated from the doing of justice, or worship used as a cover for cheating and mistreating one's neighbour, is offensive to God; indeed, the doing of justice is far more important in the eyes of God than the correct performance of the cult. Amos is typical of the prophetic tradition when he writes God's words to Israel:

'I hate, I despise your feasts,
    and I take no delight in your solemn assemblies.
Even though you offer me your burnt offerings and cereal
        offerings,
    I will not accept them,
and the peace offerings of your fatted beasts
    I will not look upon.
Take away from me the noise of your songs;
    to the melody of your harps I will not listen.

> But let justice roll down like waters,
>   and righteousness like an ever-flowing stream.'[1]

The same theme is continued in the New Testament: our relationship to God and our relationship to our neighbour are interdependent and cannot be separated without the perversion of worship. Jesus in the Sermon on the Mount puts it thus:

> 'So if you are offering your gift at the altar, and there remember that your brother has something against you, leave your gift there before the altar and go; first be reconciled to your brother, and then come and offer your gift.'[2]

Our relationships to God and to our neighbours are interdependent; they must not and cannot be separated. If Christian worship is isolated from the spheres of politics and economics, and everyday life, it loses its authenticity and easily becomes, in Marx's words, 'the opium of the people', a cover for injustice and oppression, or an irrelevance. Archbishop Trevor Huddlestone reminded us of this when he commented that too many Christians are so concerned with the real presence of Christ in the Eucharist that they forget the real presence of Christ in the needy neighbour.

Non-Christian Worship

Within the Christian tradition, some people, particularly from the 'Catholic' wing, have emphasised elements of continuity between Christian and non-Christian worship.

Christian worship is seen as the crown and fulfilment of all worship; there is no fundamental opposition between different ways of approaching God in worship, only some are less adequate than others. This attitude was shown very clearly in the letter which Pope Gregory sent to Augustine giving him guidance for his mission to the English. Augustine and his companions were counselled to take over Druidic temples, purify them and adapt them to Christian worship, and to continue in Christian form as many as possible of the rituals and customs of the people.

Worship and Idolatry

However, there is a problem involved when we turn to the Bible, for we find there a very sharp distinction drawn between true worship and idolatry. Worship which is not accompanied by, and expressed in, the doing of justice is fraudulent, even if it bears the 'right labels'; and worship of any other than the one true God is a kind of adultery, a breaking of the covenant relationship between God and God's people. Pagan worship is occasionally mentioned as allowed for Gentiles despite its basic defectiveness. For example, Naaman the Syrian, after his healing in the waters of Jordan, says to Elisha:

> 'Let there be given to your servant two mules' burden of earth; for henceforth your servant will not offer burnt offering or sacrifice to any god but the Lord. In this matter may the Lord pardon your servant: when my master goes into the house of Rimmon to worship there, leaning on my arm, and I bow myself in the house of Rimmon, ... the

Lord pardon your servant in this matter.' He said to him,
'Go in peace.'[3]

In one place, God is said to have allocated worship of the
sun and moon and stars to the pagans, but Israel is to have
nothing to do with such forms of worship.[4] Pagan worship,
the Old Testament affirms with singular consistency and
emphasis, is false, immoral, degrading and dehumanising
idolatry.

We must remember that both Jesus and the earliest
Christians continued to worship in temple and synagogue.
The New Testament sees Christian worship as the fulfilment
of Jewish worship (a point elaborated particularly in
the Epistle to the Hebrews) but in radical opposition to
Roman civil religion and all the other forms of worship in
its context. When Paul preached to the philosophers who
debated religion in Athens on the Areopagus, he declared:
'What therefore you worship as unknown, this I proclaim
to you.'[5] Paul's attitude may, in the twenty-first century,
appear to be arrogant and intolerant, but it shows the
passionate conviction he shared with the early Christians
that worship is of central and liberating importance.
Indeed, so important was this matter to the early Christians
that they were willing to die rather than burn a pinch of
incense to honour the emperor as divine. They realised
that, in worship, they were doing something of ultimate
importance, celebrating the mystery of God's love and
grace. Their passion for purity in worship was no nostalgia
for the rituals of the past, but it arose out of the excitement
of encountering the true God in worship, and finding that

their thirst for God was both satisfied and stimulated by their worship in Spirit and in Truth.

Jesus and Worship

Jesus was fully involved with the worship of Israel, and challenged the current practices of worship again and again. Jesus was taken as a baby to the temple, where he was recognised and welcomed by Simeon and Anna. As he grew to adulthood, he continued to worship.

- As a boy, he declared the temple to be 'my Father's house'.[6]
- He worshipped in the synagogue, 'as his custom was'.[7]
- He probably took part in domestic worship at table.
- He spent time in private prayer to God.

Jesus disturbed and challenged worship in word and action:

- in his cleansing of the temple
- in his words in the synagogue at Nazareth
- he prophesied the destruction of the temple
- he was accused of speaking against the temple
- he advocated a confident, joyful approach to God
- he criticised the 'heaping up of empty phrases'[8]
- he attacked the arrogance in prayer of the Pharisees
- he proclaimed that true and faithful worship demanded a passion for justice and mercy.

Worship in Spirit and in Truth

These words are from the encounter between Jesus and an unnamed Samaritan woman. She was, in every sense, an outsider. Her religious centre was in a different place. She was a woman. In addition, she was a woman with a dubious and possibly immoral past. Yet to her, Jesus says: 'God is spirit, and those who worship him must worship in spirit and truth.' Christian worship, as we explore it in this book, is the worship of God in spirit and in truth.

Questions for Discussion

1. What human needs does worship satisfy?
2. Does idolatry have any significance in the world today?
3. What is truthful worship?
4. How do we worship in spirit?

Notes

1. Amos 5:21–4.
2. Matthew 5:23–4.
3. 2 Kings 5:17–19.
4. Deuteronomy 4:15–20.
5. Acts 17:23.
6. Luke 2:49.
7. Luke 4:16.
8. Matthew 6:7.
9. John 4:20–5.

4

Worship as Play

Even when Christians speak of worship as a 'celebration', there is usually a practical stress on solemnity rather than joy and playfulness. But what if worship is a kind of play – the joyful play of the kingdom of God? It is all too easy to regard worship, liturgy (the *work* of God's people), as a serious and taxing activity, even as a form of works-righteousness, a way of striving to earn God's approval. If we are to recover the proper Christian emphasis on grace and the love of God, we should expect enjoyment and delight, even playfulness, in worship, which nonetheless takes evil and sin with great seriousness.

We need, perhaps at the start of our discussion, to remember Jesus' saying that, unless we become like little children, we shall not enter the kingdom of heaven.[1] Worshippers, even elderly ones, perhaps, should be like little children playing with eagerness and joy at the feet of the One they dare with confidence and delight to call Abba, Daddy! In worship, believers should, following the Westminster Shorter Catechism, *enjoy* God for ever. Yet some seventeenth-century Protestant dogmaticians declared that Jesus never laughed, and this was a sign of his sinlessness!

Play in the Bible

The main Protestant traditions are highly dismissive of play as a model for worship. But the Bible has plentiful descriptions of worship as an anticipation of the culmination of all things, a foretaste of the kingdom when the streets shall be full of boys and girls playing, delighting in their play and in their relationships.[2] Play is delight, wonder, enjoyment – so is worship, or so it ought to be.

Idolatry, of course, may also be play, a kind of deceitful, selfish, arrogant play, which treats earthly things as of ultimate significance, and human activity as having no space for God. Modern materialistic idolatry, in particular, tends towards the worship of Mammon or dancing round the golden calf in the desert.

The Wisdom literature in the Bible suggests that God sports with God's creation and takes delight in humanity.[3] God's rest after creation, which is reflected in the Sabbath rest of the people of God, and looks forward to the rest that God has in store for his people, is for recreation and delight, not just to renew and refresh for further work.[4] God made Leviathan to play in the deep, and the wild beasts to play on the mountains for God's delight.[5] God's people play before him. David and his men, for instance, make merry before God with all their might.[6]

So, Christian worship is not a solemn way of earning God's favour, of striving for acceptance. It should, rather, have a major dimension of grace, delight and enjoyment – as well as sensitive involvement with the problems, pain and possibilities of individuals, of the community in which we are set, and of peoples and communities far beyond our own horizons.

Play Yesterday and Today

The social scientist J. Huizinga, in his book *Homo Ludens: A Study of the Play Element in Culture* (1944), argued that play is voluntary, free and spontaneous. Play usually follows its own rules, often inexplicable to outsiders, and does not have a purpose beyond enjoyment. Play often brings everyday actions and the fantastic together through imagination. Often, it is in play that children express their interpretation of life and the puzzling world they are in. For example, it is now believed that, through play, children who have suffered traumae such as bereavement may safely express their feelings and grief and may in time be healed. The 'fun element' in play, therefore, does not exclude seriousness. Sometimes, play may be imaginative and solitary. More often, it is with others, creating and sustaining friendship.

Most of this is illuminating also as an account of Christian worship. Compulsion destroys the nature of play. Is this not also true of worship? Should worship ever be compulsory, in schools, or prisons, or in family life? There is surely a need for spontaneity and flair in playing really well – and perhaps also in praying well? In play, as in worship, rules are intended to regulate 'traffic flow' and exclude 'fouls'; but rules should not be obtrusive. You can't play squash, for example, even if you have a court, a racquet, a ball and a partner, until you know the rules. And you can't play well until the rules come naturally to you, until they are internalised. Neither play nor worship has an end beyond itself. In play, as in worship, ordinary things are put to extraordinary uses. Bread and wine in the Lord's Supper, for instance, are charged with extraordinary significance. In play, as in worship, fellowship or 'team spirit' is created, and an interpretation of life and the world is offered. And in worship, as in play, there is, or ought to be, an element of sheer delight, of enjoyment which does not exclude a profound seriousness.

Children in Church

I vividly remember the dignity and solemnity, indeed some-times what seemed like sadness, of Communion Sundays in Scotland when I was a boy. There was no Sunday school on these Communion Sundays, and we children who came to church were herded into the gallery or a side aisle to observe rather than take part in the serious celebration. We all assumed that we couldn't understand the mystery of what was happening – and that the grown-ups could!

I also remember, far later, when children were allowed in special circumstances in the Church of Scotland to receive communion, some children in our congregation asked whether they could distribute the bread and the wine, like the elders. 'Of course you can't – you're too young' was the considered reply. At which a boy of about ten challenged the minister: 'But Jesus took bread and fish from a wee boy and passed it round for everyone.'[7] The minister's sophisticated theology made a lateral shift in the face of such simplicity –

and, the following Easter, the children, watched somewhat nervously by hovering elders, distributed the bread and the wine to the congregation with great reverence and almost palpable joy.

Another World

In play, we can anticipate the future and enter a different world, like the children going through the wardrobe into Narnia in C. S. Lewis's book, *The Lion, the Witch and the Wardrobe*. There, in this different world, we practise in play the roles that we hope that we will fulfil in the future.

Years ago while holidaying in the north of Scotland, we stopped with our two children on the banks of a loch to have a picnic. While the children played nearby, we read, drowsed, enjoyed the scenery. When we decided it was time to move on, we discovered that the children were in another world. The boulders, the heather and the birch trees now made for them the rooms of a house – the kitchen, the bedroom and so forth. In this setting, they were playing out the roles of a mum and a dad, or being farmers, fishermen and so on. In the next instant, it had all changed to be a Robin Hood-type fantasy with 'baddies' out there, and the two of them holding the torch for honour, truth and justice. They were chattering all the time, totally engrossed in acting out a drama which was clearly anticipating roles they expected to play in later life, preparing them for the future. Similarly in worship, Christians practise for their roles in God's kingdom. What is done and what is said in worship should be a preparation for truthful, just and loving action in the world in all the days to come.

In an Edinburgh church, I started a campaign to discourage the elders from dressing for communion in their funereal wear – black tie and sober suits. Communion, I asserted, is not a wake for a dead God. Then a wonderful, warm and profoundly Christian elder took me aside and said:

> Duncan, you don't understand. During the bad years of the Depression, my family lived in real poverty. My father was a labourer in the docks. He was an elder of the Kirk. The owner of the shipyard was an elder in the same Kirk Session. It meant everything to my father that he and the owner of the yard, dressed in striped trousers and morning coat, walked down the aisle together, carrying the elements. Often, that suit would be back in the pawn-broker's if the work wasn't there. But we *always* redeemed it for communion. That way, the boss and my father were equal.

I learned from that good man that, in worship, we foretell the equality of the kingdom. Although I persisted in my campaign to make communion attire more celebratory, I learned a valuable and humbling lesson.

In worship, then, we enter another world, God's world, a world of mystery. And what we do and say in Christian worship should express the beauty, love and equality of God's kingdom. But we are not escaping from this world, with all its ambiguities, conflicts and suffering. Worship is also a stage, so that others may see, in what we say and do, a little of what the kingdom of God is like, and be invited to join in playing a role in God's great drama.

Playtime is Storytime

Stories tell us who we are, where we belong, what our responsibilities are, and what is our destiny. Stories are tremendously important. And storytelling is at the heart of Christian worship.

As a small boy in St Andrews, I used to pester my mother every time we passed a certain ancient house to tell me the stories of Willie Douglas. He had been a pageboy to Mary Queen of Scots. In later life, he had lived in that house, so close to my home. Willie had gone with Mary when she was imprisoned on an island in Loch Leven. He it was who had stolen the key to the castle from the drunk governor, and ushered the queen out to a waiting boat, with horses on the shore to take her to freedom. I often wondered why that story was so important to me. And then it became clear. Willie Douglas, had been, like me, a young boy. He had done a brave and noble deed, and in later life he had become part of the same community as me – the little city of St Andrews. His story and my story were in a sense blended.

In worship, our stories and God's great story are grafted together. The stories of the kingdom and the parables of Jesus tell us who we are.

In the Jewish Passover, the definitive story of the Exodus is retold and re-enacted ritually. The youngest child present, representing those who are not yet formed, who have not received an identity, who have not yet heard and re-enacted the story often enough or in sufficiently different ways for it to have shaped their self-understanding, asks four key questions.

- Why does this night differ from all other nights? For, on all other nights, we eat either leavened or unleavened bread; why on this night only unleavened bread?
- On all other nights, we eat all kinds of herbs; why on this night only bitter herbs?
- On all other nights, we need not dip our herbs even once; why on this night must we dip them twice?
- On all other nights, we eat either sitting or reclining; why on this night do we all recline?

The reply from the elders comes in terms of the story of the first Passover and of God's deliverance of his people from Egypt, the story which they are ritually re-enacting, and the story which tells the child and the whole gathering what it means to be a Jew.

> We were Pharaoh's slaves in Egypt, and the Lord our God brought us forth with a mighty hand and an outstretched arm. And if the Holy One, Blessed be He, had not brought our forefathers forth from Egypt, then we, our children, and our children's children, would still be slaves in Egypt. So, even though all of us were wise, all of us full of understanding, all of us elders, all of us knowing the Torah, we should still be under the commandment to tell the story of the departure from Egypt. And the more one tells the story of the departure from Egypt, the more praiseworthy he is.[8]

And that is precisely what happens at the Passover feast. They tell again the old story, they sing and pray about it, they discuss it, but above all they re-enact the first Passover meal, appropriating afresh the story of God's deliverance and making it live in contemporary experience.

The Passover reminds us of another central characteristic of all worship in the historical religions of Judaism, Christianity and Islam: in worship, we find our place in time and understand the present moment by looking back and by looking forward. In worship, we look back in order to understand ourselves and our times; we must hear again and relate ourselves to the stories of God's dealings with his people. We need constantly to repossess our past as something that is still operative and influential in the present. And, in this process, we see where we 'fit in'. Just as children delight to hear the story of their births and early days, of events of which they have no memory, and to hear about their parents' childhood, so in worship we need to hear the living voice of the past telling us tales which shape us by showing us who we are and how we came to be here.

The stories of the past are like powerful searchlights probing into the future, flooding with light the dark corners of our souls, our communities, our world. So, in the 'play' of worship, in hearing again the stories of the past, the present comes alive. This may stimulate us to pray for and work for the last and the least and the lost. So, worship both educates worshippers and challenges them to service and generosity. These stories challenge us to faithful and generous action, the action of God's kingdom.

Team Games

In Christian worship, in living and loving the mystery, we are never alone. We have been chosen to be part of God's team in heaven and on earth – the communion of saints. In team games, play creates and strengthens relationships: we learn to depend on one another and to work together as part of the team. The life of faith is a kind of relay race, according to the Letter to the Hebrews. The baton of faith is handed on from one generation to the next. Those who have run the race of faith before us now form a 'great cloud of witnesses', our fans, who cheer us on as we run our lap in the great race of faith. And the saints of the past who encourage us today, we are told, will not reach their perfection or win the race without us.[9]

In due course, we hand on our baton to those who come afterwards. We do our best – but we do not do it by ourselves or for ourselves. Our work is not, and never can be, complete. With joy, we pass on the baton and watch the race continuing to be run by those who come after us.

Training – for God's Future

If you play tennis, or football or cricket, or any sport, you need to get into training, or else your play will let the side down. If worship is a kind of play – the play of the kingdom – we need to get into training lest we let down our side and ourselves. The writer of the Epistle to the Hebrews puts it thus:

Therefore, since we are surrounded by so great a cloud of witnesses, let us also lay aside every weight, and sin which clings so closely, and let us run with perseverance the race that is set before us, looking to Jesus the pioneer and perfecter of our faith, who for the joy that was set before him endured the cross, despising the shame, and is seated at the right hand of the throne of God.[10]

Training may be hard, and sometimes painful, but it is necessary if we are to achieve our goals and operate as effective members of the team – God's team.

Questions for Discussion

1. In what ways may the playful worship of the Church anticipate the worship of heaven?

2. Is speaking of Christian worship as a form of play a little frivolous?

3. Why are stories so important for Christian faith – as distinct from ethical injunctions, for example?

4. In what specific ways may Christians get into 'training'?

Notes

1. Matthew 18:3.
2. Zechariah 8:5; Isaiah 11:8 etc.
3. Proverbs 8:25–31.
4. Hebrews 4:1ff.
5. Psalm 104:26; Job 40:20.
6. 2 Samuel 6:5; 1 Chronicles 13:8.

7. John 6:9.
8. Nahum N. Glatzer (ed.), *The Passover Haggadah* (New York: Schocken Books, 1953).
9. Hebrews 11:39–40.
10. Hebrews 12:1–2.

5

Washings

Washing is a significant part of everyone's life, but we don't often think about it. Traditionally, a new-born baby is washed soon after delivery. And, just after death, a corpse is washed or cleaned in preparation for burial or cremation. In between birth and death, there are countless washings in everyone's life – washing hands before meals; regular baths or showers each day to keep the body clean and healthy. Then there are luxury washings, in the sauna or the spa. The basic ingredient of washings is water; but, along with water, usually soap and oils of various sorts are used in washing. Soon after I first arrived in India, the old man who cooked my meals told me that, in the great heat of India, in addition to 'water bath', one needed to have, once a week at least, an 'oil bath' to keep the skin healthy and supple. And he was right.

We adults wash ourselves, but we also wash our children and sometimes our elderly relatives who are too frail to wash themselves. Bathtime with children is usually great fun. And one thing that the children learn in the bath is the importance of keeping clean. Being dirty is dangerous because of infections that flourish in dirt. In the bath, children relax in the warm water, and they come to know the love of their parents and the need to avoid dirt and infection. And old or sick folk being bathed by carers or relatives are aware that the bath conveys a message of love, affection and care.

Religion and Washing

Most religions have a strong emphasis on washing. As we have already seen, in a typical Hindu temple, the deity is awakened with music in the morning, and then washed, and offered food, before allowing the worshippers, who have also washed in preparation, to have *darshan*, or audience of their god. Worshippers of most faiths expect to wash as a central part of their preparation for worship.

Several years ago, my wife and I were walking outside Kodaikanal in the hills of southern India. Across a small valley, in a lonely hill village, it appeared to us as though all the women and all the children were out by a burn, washing and scrubbing their clothes. Sarees, trousers, lungis and djibbahs, all white, were laid out on the ground to dry and bleach in the sun. Then we remembered that the next day was Pentecost. Clearly, this village was Christian; clothes as well as bodies had to be clean for the celebration!

To approach God, one should be as pure as possible, inwardly and outwardly. The physical washing reflects an inner, spiritual washing and purification and a proper respect for the deity.

Judaism was no exception to this rule. The Old Testament is full of regulations and ordinances about washing as an essential part of the approach to Jahweh in prayer and worship. Leviticus in particular is replete with detailed

regulations about washing and purification. In contrast, it is
notable that Jesus and his disciples acquired the reputation
of being careless about the regulations concerning washings.
They were accused of disregarding the rituals of cleaning and
of washing enjoined in the Torah, and of breaking through
the barriers between the pure and the polluted, the unclean.
They were criticised for not taking seriously the tradition on
these matters.[1] They, in their turn, suggested that the scribes
and Pharisees were obsessed with rules and regulations about
washings at the expense of taking seriously the weightier
matters of the law – theft, murder, adultery, . . . envy, slander,
pride.[2]

Baptism: John and Jesus

Jesus' cousin, John, established a movement that called on
all people to repent of their sins and be baptised as a sign
that their sins were forgiven, or washed away, and that they
were now enrolled in a movement in which all sorts of
people together sought to prepare the way for the coming
Messiah and the New Age that he would inaugurate. There
was a strong atmosphere of expectation, and great numbers
of people flocked to be baptised by John in the River Jordan
and to enrol themselves in John's movement of expectation,
hope and commitment.

When Jesus came to John and asked to be baptised, John
hesitated: 'I need to be baptized by you, and do you come to
me?'[3] Jesus insisted, and John consented. 'And when Jesus
was baptized, he went up immediately from the water, and
behold, the heavens were opened and he saw the Spirit of

God descending like a dove, and alighting on him; and lo, a voice from heaven, saying, "This is my Beloved Son, with whom I am well pleased."[4] For Jesus, as for all baptised by John, and for all baptised since then, baptism was not only a ceremonial washing but also the reception of a new identity and enrolment in a new community of expectant faith. But the new identity, even for Jesus, was not easy and simple, as he discovered when he went into the wilderness and was tempted by the Devil.

Can you imagine how his baptism by his cousin, a crucial event just before the start of his ministry, ignited in Jesus' mind the great question 'Who am I?' and drove him to the wilderness to seek an answer? He wanted to be alone. But he could not be at peace. There in the wilderness, Jesus felt the fear of the future. He doubted his capacity to fulfil his Father's call. He did not find it easy to obey. He wrestled with who he was, and with whether he had the capacity to undertake the huge task that God had set before him.

'Who am I?' Jesus asked:

- A magician, manufacturing wonder and amazement?
- An immortal, who will never die or suffer?
- An emperor, revered and feared by all?

These were real temptations, even for God's Son, the Beloved, in whom God takes delight. And even at the end, on the cross, Jesus, I believe, was haunted by the question: 'Who am I? Does it all make sense?' On the cross, he cried in despair: 'My God, my God, why have you forsaken me?'[5] He must have asked: 'Who am I? – the God-forsaken One?'

And you and I – again and again we ask the question 'Who am I?' And we want a clear, simple answer. But it seldom comes like that. Sometimes we do a lot of play-acting, pretending to be someone we are not, giving quite dishonest answers to the insistent question 'Who am I?' We may give way to temptations, to pride or arrogance. Then again, we may find it hard to recognise the vocation God has for us, denying God's gracious love and generosity. 'Who am I?' is a question we all must face. When we turn to Jesus, we are encountering One who has been tested and tempted like us, who constantly cries: 'Who am I?'

Jesus, we read in the gospel, referred to his coming sufferings as his baptism. And the baptism of Christians is often understood as baptism into the death of Christ:

> Do you not know that all of us who have been baptized into Christ Jesus were baptized into his death? We were buried therefore with him by baptism into death, so that as Christ was raised from the dead by the glory of the Father, we too might walk in newness of life.[6]

This same Jesus, far later, on the evening before his arrest, met with his disciples at Passover time for a festive meal. At the end of the meal, he stripped for action and insisted on washing his disciples' feet – normally the role of the humblest servant. When he had completed the washing, he told his disciples that they ought to wash one another's feet, 'for I have given you an example, that you also should do as I have done to you'.[7] Washing of the feet was the epitome of humble service and the model of what discipleship should involve. His ceremonial washing of the disciples' feet by the One who was their Lord and Master offered a model of the disciples' task as ministry, humble service of the weak and the poor, the 'unclean' and the forgotten.

Baptism and Washing in the Early Church

Baptism was quickly established as the ritual of entry into the Jesus movement. Think of the wonderful story of the day of Pentecost recorded in Acts 2, delighting in the great list of countries and cities from which the respondents to the gospel came, and the fact that they all heard the good news in their own languages:

> Parthians, Medes, Elamites, and residents of Mesopotamia, Judea and Cappadocia, Pontus and Asia, Phrygia and Pamphylia, Egypt and the parts of Libya belonging to Cyrene, and visitors from Rome, both Jews and proselytes, Cretans and Arabs – in our own languages we hear them speaking about God's deeds of power.[8]

Here, surely, we have the birthday of the Church, a fellowship in which people – women and men – are accepted on the basis of their faith and their baptism, not their birth, status, purity, achievements or ethnic origin. Here, surely, was a Church in which worldly distinctions were set aside, a new kind of inclusive community, in which baptism was the entry to a fellowship of believers who had been washed and were now members of a radically new kind of community.

Or was it? We are told that the crowd was composed of 'devout Jews from every nation under heaven living in

Jerusalem'.[9] They were Jews by birth, or Jews by choice – in most cases, probably both! Peter addresses the crowd as 'Men of Judea and all who live in Jerusalem' and as 'You that are Israelites', and he concludes his address with these words: 'Therefore let *the entire house of Israel* know with certainty that God has made him both Lord and Messiah, this Jesus whom you crucified.'[10] Is the significance of what happened on the first Christian Pentecost contained within the broad boundaries of Judaism, defended by rules about purity and pollution, what you may eat and whom you may eat and drink with, who can be baptised and who should be denied baptism?

It perhaps appears that the drama of the first Pentecost took place within the limits of Jewry, and that the whole *dramatis personae* on that occasion was Jewish. One might perhaps at that wonderful moment in history have assumed that the Church was called and destined to grow and flourish and witness in and to Jewry, as a Jewish sect, without reaching out to the poor and the rejected among Gentiles, or indeed to the powerful Gentiles such as centurions or magistrates, or soldiers, or businesswomen such as Lydia, the first Christian in Europe – even those Gentiles who oppressed the faithful! Is it perhaps possible that ethnic barriers are more difficult to overcome than those within a specific religious community?

On the face of it, the barriers of purity and pollution that kept Jew and Gentile apart were not challenged on the first Christian Pentecost. Perhaps these boundaries of purity and pollution are the most difficult of all to transcend. Yet, the prophecy that Peter quotes from the Hebrew Scriptures is about the outpouring of the Spirit 'upon *all flesh*' – not just on the Jews, or on the pure folk.[11]

It would be foolish nonetheless to underestimate the significance of the fact that, on that first Pentecost day, the hearers all heard the good news in their mother tongues. The gospel *can* overcome cultural divisions and heal the confusion and misunderstanding of Babel. Real understanding between people of different languages is not easy. But it is possible. My Indian students warmed to me as soon as they knew that I was seriously studying the Tamil language and trying to speak in Tamil. They had had the experience of struggling with English in order to communicate, and they knew that studying a foreign language is not an easy task, but often it is necessary.

Divisions of language are not as deep and resistant as divisions which proclaim that some people by virtue of their birth are pure, and others are irremediably impure. The first Pentecost seemed to spread, like the ripples in a pond when a stone is thrown. The initiative here, it is clear, was the Spirit's. In the first stage, Philip goes to preach in Samaria.[12] The people of this religiously rather deviant community – not quite Jewish, not quite Gentile – eagerly accepted the gospel and were baptised. Then, Peter and John were sent by the apostles, presumably to find out and assess what was happening in Samaria. They recognised that the Spirit was now indeed at work among the Samaritans. After Peter and John had prayed and laid their hands on them, the Samaritans too received the Spirit.

The next stage is more dramatic, as recounted in Acts 10. The Spirit leads; and Peter, kicking and screaming as it were, follows. The issue here is unambiguously purity and pollution, and who may be washed in baptism. This issue is also central to the nature of the Christian Church. It is an issue that has plagued the Church down the ages and still causes trouble today. Peter is confronted with the direct challenge: the voice in the dream declares to him authoritatively: 'What God has made clean, you must not call profane.'[13] The issue, of course, is about more than food. It is about the people with whom we may have fellowship. It is about the people we can call sisters and brothers. It is about the nature of the Church of Jesus Christ. It is about our response to the leading of the Spirit. It is about obedience.

The story does not end in Joppa. What happened there was reported to the Church leaders in Jerusalem, and they recognised and acknowledged the leading of the Spirit, which enabled the mission to the Gentiles. But even Peter from time to time remained reluctant, uneasy about breaking free from the old boundaries which gave a kind of security. His initial response, 'I have never eaten anything that is profane or unclean',[14] recurs again and again as the story is re-enacted down the years.

And the same is true with Paul. Immediately after his conversion, while Paul is in a trance, Jesus says to him: 'Go, for I will send you far away to the Gentiles.'[15] Again and again, Paul declares he is turning to the Gentiles, sometimes embracing the broader Pentecostal vision, sometimes in sheer frustration at the lack of response from Jews.[16]

All down the ages, in every culture and society, the Church has struggled with the call to be faithful in its mission, to realise its true nature, in which the barriers of pollution and suspicion and hostility between people are overcome. Often, there have been hesitations and compromises. But the call is persistent and the Spirit breaks down barriers, again and again, and calls on Christians to manifest in baptism the Pentecostal community in which 'There is no longer Jew or Greek, there is no longer slave or free, there is no longer male or female; for all of you are one in Christ Jesus.'[17]

Only in this way may the Church be indeed the sign of the coming unity of humankind, and a manifestation of the reconciliation wrought in Christ. And, in that Church, all the baptised will be welcome to eat and drink at the same table without fear of pollution, contempt or disgrace.

Questions for Discussion

1. What was, and is, the continued significance of Jesus washing his disciples' feet?
2. Can Christian baptism change social and economic divisions?
3. Are there unacknowledged barriers within our own church?

Notes

1. Mark 7:1–8.
2. Mark 7:1–23.
3. Matthew 3:14.
4. Matthew 3:16–17.
5. Matthew 27:46 (NRSV); Psalm 22:1 (NRSV).
6. Romans 6:3–4.

7. John 13:15.
8. Acts 2:9–11 (NRSV).
9. Acts 2:5 (NRSV).
10. Acts 2:14, 22 and 36 (NRSV).
11. Acts 2:17 (NRSV); cf. Joel 2:28.
12. Acts 8:4–8.
13. Acts 10:15 (NRSV).
14. Acts 10:14 (NRSV).
15. Acts 22:21 (NRSV).
16. Acts 13:46–8, 18:6.
17. Galatians 3:28 (NRSV).

Baptism and Society

Baptism and Pollution: The Indian Case

In many societies, whole categories of people even today are regarded as impure and polluting. The millions in India who are now called Dalits used to be known as Untouchables, irremediably polluting to everyone from the higher, 'purer' castes.

Even today in rural southern India, after the monsoon, the emerald-green paddy fields are alive with labourers, women in bright sarees, bent double over the rice fields. The men will work hard and long in the searing heat on the land or in quarries or at road-mending. The workers for the most part will be Dalits, the people called 'outcastes' in times past. Today, despite all the political rhetoric and the legislation to improve the lot of the 'scheduled castes', they are the poorest of the poor, in most places forced to live in squalid settlements of their own outside the main village, despised, exploited, excluded and oppressed. Usually they even have their own water supply, often not piped, separate from the high-caste people.

If a Dalit labourer needs a drink, he must walk towards the high-caste landlord's house, stop some safe distance away, and call out that he is thirsty. Soon, a young high-caste woman will emerge from the house, carrying a clay vessel, or *cujah*, of water. Carefully avoiding any touch or physical contact, she will pour the water into the Dalit's cupped hands, and watch as he laps the water, pouring more as required. She will then retire, her ritual purity still intact, to the house. Had the Dalit touched the *cujah*, it would need to be destroyed. Had he entered the Brahmin house, the whole building would require to be purified and washed. Had there been physical contact, however incidental, however trivial, between the young woman and the Dalit, she would have to go through an elaborate ritual of purification, of washing.

Christianity first came to India in the early centuries, reputedly brought by St Thomas the Apostle, who was later believed to have been martyred at Mylapore near Chennai (Madras). The Syrian Christian Church, the first church in India, quickly established itself as a high-status 'pure' community allocated an elevated position in the social hierarchy, encapsulated within the caste system, not seeking converts – particularly from low-caste groups. Far later, some early missionaries, such as Roberto de Nobili in the seventeenth century, made converts among the Brahmins and other high-status communities and accommodated themselves without difficulty or serious question into the caste system. Later, nineteenth-century missionaries of various traditions questioned whether caste, with its strict rules about purity and pollution and washing, was compatible with Christianity and Christian baptism. The churches were riven with controversies on this account. The problem continues to cause dissension and division in the Indian Church today.

Things are of course changing in India as elsewhere, but the whole business of purity and pollution, of dirt and washing, is astonishingly deep-seated, in different ways and in different contexts. A dear friend and academic colleague of mine, a devout Hindu, is the traditional headman of a small village deep in the countryside, where tradition dies hard. He was opposed to caste and was outraged at the poverty and degradation that most Dalits have to suffer on a daily basis. He identified a number of promising young Dalit men from his village, and enrolled them in the college and paid their fees. In college he was a father to them; he ate with them without a second thought, and they could chat freely. But, when we visited his village, these same students could not enter the headman's house, but had to stand outside in the heat and wait for us to join them there.

Although these people were Hindu, such distinctions of purity and pollution survive in the Indian Church to this very day. The frontier between different denominations or parishes often reflects old caste distinctions between the 'pure' and the 'impure'. For many years, few Christians of low-caste origin were ordained, and those who were ordained were frequently not accepted by Christians of high-caste origin, particularly as ministers of the Church's meal, the Eucharist. When, in 1739, it was proposed in southern India to ordain one Rajanaiken, a catechist of low-caste origins, some of the SPCK/Lutheran missionaries protested that Rajanaiken, although useful as a catechist, could not be ordained. They believed that, if converts of high-caste origin saw Rajanaiken administering the Lord's Supper, they would begin to have less respect for the sacrament.

The sacramental elements, in their view, would be polluted by the hands of a low-caste person, a fellow Christian and a priest, however valid his baptism and his ordination. Interestingly, this was precisely the same theological reasoning which was used in Scotland against the ordination of women in the 1960s.

In similar manner, in many cases, arrangements were made for Christians of pure- and impure-caste origins to be segregated in church, in one case in southern India walls being erected so that the priest could go to the altar in a kind of tunnel, and neither group could see the other even when receiving communion at the altar rails! Again and again, the Church in India allowed itself to give way to caste tradition and prejudices.

But there is a more positive outcome arising from this issue. Specifically because many Christians were able to transcend the fears of pollution that were so deeply entrenched in Hindu culture, a hugely disproportionate number of Christians from the Indian subcontinent were able to enter caring professions such as nursing without fear of losing their purity by serving the basic human and physical needs of their sick neighbours.

Baptism, Race and Caste

It was not only among Indians, of course, that accommodation with traditional fears of pollution persisted. Some

Europeans in India, who proclaimed that converts must not hesitate to share the Lord's Supper with those whom they had previously thought polluting, rarely if ever sat down at the common table to eat with Indian friends. Missionaries and other Europeans were accused time and again of a subtle, perhaps unconscious, racist prejudice, and of refusing to acknowledge that in the West there were versions of social order and fears of pollution which were quite as deep-seated, un-Christian and objectionable as caste.

It was precisely this assumption, that European forms of hierarchy were in no way in tension with the gospel, which was challenged by a few Indian Christians and missionaries who rightly divined the radical and far-reaching implications of the opposition to caste. 'The West', wrote C. F. Andrews, 'must not try to pull the mote out of India's eye while the beam remains in its own eye.'[1] The Church, he argued, can only succeed if it refuses to harbour within itself the racial and caste evils from which India is longing to be free.[2] Andrews and like-minded missionaries and Indian Christians believed that the Christian critique of caste was also a critique of class and of racism, and of the degradation and division engendered by a great gulf between rich and poor, upper and lower class, the powerful and the weak in the West. They drew attention to the fact that class had frequently been taught as God-given in the Christian West.

Indian Christians pushed the argument one stage further, suggesting that any class system, especially the British class system, must be called into question as much as the Indian caste system. Inherited land, wealth and position do not lie easily within the Christian gospel.

Baptism and the Irish Troubles

Huge and perplexing issues still surround questions of washing and baptism in the Christian Church today. At the height of the 'Troubles' in Northern Ireland, a leading Roman Catholic theologian, Father Enda McDonagh, reminded us that baptism as incorporation into the dying and rising of Christ is baptism into the *one* Church, which is the body of Christ. This is not a purely legal point – that different denominations accept the validity of baptismal initiation into membership – but it goes far deeper. In our divisions, or rather, despite our divisions, we all share in Christ. The celebration of a baptism involves, he argues, not only the congregation, denomination or confession in which it takes place, but also all the other Christian communities. Only in this way is it capable of signifying credibly the coming unity of all humankind.

There was a time when Enda McDonagh declared that one way forward to heal factions and divisions and sectarianism in Northern Ireland was to stop baptising. This was certainly a shock tactic, but it had good theology at its core. In Northern Ireland, baptism, whether in a Protestant church or a Roman Catholic church, had become seen by many as entry into a social and political community. The social and political significance of baptism was perceived as being greater than the theological assertion that baptism is into Jesus Christ, entry into the one, holy, catholic and apostolic church. While baptism was seen thus, McDonagh claimed that ceasing to practise baptism may be a way for people of faith to move forward together.

McDonagh's suggestion arises out of a passion that the authentic meaning and significance of baptism should shine forth, and an awareness that distortion often enters in. In the baptismal liturgy of my own church, the parents are enjoined to unfold to the children who have been baptised the mystery and wonder and treasure they have been given, and to enter into it for themselves. We should all be concerned with the constant unfolding of the ethical and spiritual treasure that is given to us in baptism, in Eucharist and in the proclamation of the gospel.

One Baptism

From the beginning, baptism has been the rite of entry into the One, Holy and Apostolic Church, the Christian community. It is a sign of belonging to the communion of saints, the one holy Church on earth in which we are all responsible for one another and to one another. The seventeenth-century poet and preacher, John Donne, put it thus:

> The Church is Catholike, universal, so are all her Actions; All that she does, belongs to *all*, when she baptises a child, that action concerns mee; for that child is thereby connected to that Head which is my Head too, and engraffed into that *body*, whereof I am a *member*. And when she buries a Man that action concerns me; All mankind is of one *Author*, and is one *volume*.[3]

In more recent times in Scotland, a baptismal certificate with an interesting symbol at the top was much used in the Church of Scotland. Looked at one way, the symbol was a thistle – Scotland's national flower – at the top; looked at another way, it was a dove descending. But, whatever way one looked at it, the symbol was unambiguously tartan! Mercifully, that certificate has been withdrawn and replaced by a properly ecumenical alternative.

Infant Baptism or Believers' Baptism?

For many centuries, there has been vigorous debate about whether Christian baptism can be rightly administered to infants as well as to adults. The supporters of the baptism of infants suggest that it expresses well the pure grace of God in Christ, when an infant who has neither achievements to boast of, nor sins to be forgiven, is washed in baptism and received into the Christian community. Baptism of infants was a little like circumcision among Jews, although baptism from the beginning was of girls as well as boys. When we read of 'households' being baptised, it presumably includes children as well as the adult members of the household. In the age of Christendom, it was generally assumed that all children would be baptised soon after birth as a kind of routine declaration that they were members of the Christian community, the Una Sancta.

In the Orthodox tradition, babies on baptism receive the sacramental elements as a sign that they are fully received into the Church. In the Syrian Orthodox baptismal service in southern India, the priest takes the sacrament very seriously. No perfunctory sprinkling of a drop of water here! The priest rolls the sleeves of his vestments up to the elbow and receives the first child from the arms of his

father. The font is like a large baby bath. The children sit
in it while the priest splashes blessed baptismal water all
over the child – the arms, the legs, the head and the body.
The priest then pours oil on his hands and anoints the
baptised children one by one, boys first and then the girls.
The children are then returned to their fathers' arms, and
receive communion in the form of a tiny morsel of bread
and a drop or two of wine. Infants they may be, but they
are now recognised as full members of the household of
God. Is this the working-out of Jesus' saying, 'Let the little
children come to me, and do not stop them; for it is to such
as these that the kingdom of God belongs. Truly I tell you,
whoever does not receive the kingdom of God as a little
child will never enter it'?[4]

In the Roman Catholic tradition, children take their
first communion around the age of seven, seen as an age
of accountability. The other traditions that practise infant
baptism as the norm encourage children during the teenage
years to confirm the faith confessed by the Church on
their behalf at baptism. They are then admitted to the full
responsibilities and privileges of the Christian Church.

In the Church of Scotland's *Common Order*, the words
in the order for infant baptism, borrowed from the French
Reformed Church's order, affirm that in baptism we rely on
the grace of God along with the promises of the parents. The
minister addresses the child:

N...,
for you Jesus Christ came into the world,
for you he lived and showed God's love;

for you he suffered the darkness of Calvary
and cried at the last, 'It is accomplished';
for you he triumphed over death
and rose in newness of life;
for you he ascended to reign at God's right hand.
All this he did for you, N. . .,
though you do not know it yet.
And so the word of Scripture is fulfilled:
'We love because God loved us first.'[5]

And, in the Order for the Baptism of Adults, these words are to be found:

In this sacrament,
the love of God
is offered to each one of us.
Though we cannot understand or explain it,
we are called to accept that love
with the openness and trust of a child.[6]

Baptism is a mystery to be lived and loved, whether administered to an adult or to a baby. And perhaps the adult and the child are together in *not* understanding the mystery but rejoicing in it.

Questions for Discussion

1. Should baptism be only of adult believers?
2. What are the arguments for and against the baptism of infants?
3. Can Christian baptism promote social equality?

Notes

1. C. F. Andrews, *The True India: A Plea for Understanding* (London, 1939), p. 151.
2. C. F. Andrews, *The Renaissance in India* (London, 1912), pp. 188–9.
3. Devotions XVII, in John Donne, *Complete Poems and Selected Prose* (London, 1945).
4. Luke 18:16–17 (NRSV).
5. *Book of Common Order of the Church of Scotland* (Edinburgh: Saint Andrew Press, 1994), pp. 89–90.
6. *Common Order*, p. 99.

7

Eating and Drinking with Jesus

The Meals Jesus Shared

In the 1980s, Rabbi Lionel Blue and Canon John Elvey produced a splendid cookery book. It was more than a collection of recipes; it was full of family anecdotes and stories pointing up the differences and similarities between the Judaic and Christian religions. An introductory letter from the rabbi tells how he felt welcomed into the canon's home as a guest, but, when he was allowed into the kitchen, he felt they were friends. Most people know that feeling. The kitchen is the heart of the home. The rabbi goes on to explain that he had not read the gospels while growing up, only coming to them as an adult. He was bowled over by their domesticity, their Jewishness and the near-obsession with eating and cooking! Perhaps because we Christians have been brought up with the gospels, we forget how domestic and culinary they are. Rabbi Blue was delighted to read of the meals Jesus had with Mary and Martha and Lazarus, of the supper parties with sinners, not to mention the wedding that ran out of wine. And the rabbi confesses that he began to see why the central act of Christian worship is in fact a supper.

Is there any biography which tells us as much about its subject's eating and drinking as the gospels do about Jesus? Here was a man who was a lover of food and drink and of human company. He ate with his disciples – and what a mixed bunch they were! He ate with Zacchaeus, and with Levi. He ate with Pharisees and with quislings. A woman of the streets came in and washed his feet and spoke with him while he was at table. Is it surprising that he acquired a reputation, not as a holy man, not as a gloomy ascetic, but as one who enjoyed eating and drinking? But what really shocked the religious folk of his time was that Jesus was happy to share his table-fellowship with prostitutes and traitors and other notorious sinners. He shared with outcasts, with people whom everyone despised and feared. 'Look, a glutton and a drunkard, a friend of tax-collectors and sinners!'[1]

Jesus also told stories about meals: the people invited to the banquet who invented excuses not to come and whose places were taken by people off the streets, the great feast to welcome back the prodigal son, the coming feast in the kingdom of heaven. And, when he found himself in the country, far from any village, surrounded by crowds of hungry and confused people – the sheep without a shepherd, he called them – he fed them because he was moved with compassion for them.

As Jesus faced the imminence of betrayal, suffering and death, at Passover time in Jerusalem, he gathered his disciples around him to eat a meal together in the upper room. It was a traditional Jewish festival meal, now a meal linked for ever to his death and resurrection. He wanted to share his agony and his foreboding with his friends. He wanted their encouragement and support. After supper, he washed his disciples' feet. Yet, after that meal, Judas betrayed him. Peter denied him. 'Then all the disciples deserted him and fled.'[2]

There were meals after the resurrection, table-fellowship with the risen Lord. In John's Gospel, the disciples have been fishing all night without catching anything. In the misty dawn, a shadowy figure by a charcoal fire on the shore shouts to them some suggestions for their fishing. Then he says: 'Come and have breakfast'. And there, as they eat their picnic meal, 'they knew it was the Lord'.[3] On the Emmaus road, in a story from Luke,[4] the two disciples who had been so engrossed with their own worries and fears recognise Jesus when the stranger takes bread, blesses it, breaks it and gives it to them: 'he had been made known to them in the breaking of the bread'.[5] From this resurrection story, the Church of South India has taken these words for a communion prayer: 'Be present, be present, Jesus, good High Priest, as you were with your disciples, and make yourself known to us in the breaking of the bread.'

The Meal Jesus Gave to Us

From the resurrection until today, Christians have gathered Sunday by Sunday to enjoy fellowship with the Lord at his table. Our earliest evidence is from Paul, particularly the passage in 1 Corinthians 11. Before Paul wrote these words to the church in Corinth, the disciples in Jerusalem 'devoted themselves to the apostles' teaching and fellowship, to the breaking of bread and the prayers'.'[6] What we do in our church or meeting house, chapel or cathedral, is continuous with that meal. It is at the heart of the Christian life. Here, Christians meet in a special way with their Lord, around the meal table. Here, they have fellowship with him. Here, he makes himself known to them in the breaking of the bread.

We gather at a table which is not our table but the Lord's. It is not the Church's supper but the Lord's Supper. That's why there is a place at this table for people like us, for sinners, for people who are failures, for people who lack confidence and make mistakes. In fact, that's the kind of people for whom it exists. At this table, there is a place for outcasts, for people who are despised, for people whom we may even fear. There is a place for handicapped people, people with AIDS, homeless people, prisoners. We cannot have fellowship with the Lord without being open to the kind of people for whom he has a special care. That's the company he likes to keep.

This is a meal for hungry people, for needy people, for people who are hungry for God, for love, for forgiveness, for acceptance, for peace. It's the kind of meal that both satisfies and promises more. It whets our appetite.

In the Lord's Supper, we deal with material things, bread and wine, as we ought to deal with all God's good gifts to us. We delight in them. We treat them with reverence. We do not waste or guzzle. We use them to express our love for one another; we share them. We enjoy them. We give thanks for them, for the bread and for the wine, for the love and the suffering that they signify – and for all God's goodness.

This is a place and a time for festivity, for joy and for laughter. It is a party for God's children, playing at the feet of Abba, Daddy, our father.

Rabbi Blue was right when he came to the conclusion that the central act of Christian worship is a meal. And the atmosphere and themes of this meal should transform our ordinary meals and transfigure the whole of our life.

Word Made Flesh Made Bread

This is what God did. The Word became flesh in Jesus the Christ. The mystery of the universe lay in the manger as a tiny, helpless baby, bone of our bone and flesh of our flesh. The message that people couldn't and wouldn't hear when it was delivered by the prophets became a person, Jesus. It was Jesus who showed us, in his life and suffering as well as in his teaching, the mystery of God's love for us. This is the trysting place and the touching place given to us where we touch and handle things unseen, the very mystery of the universe incarnate in Jesus. He is the host at the table, offering forgiveness, giving encouragement, meeting us for our delight. This is mystery in the commonplace. This is what God did.

That's why, in the Christian tradition, people have always taught that Word and Sacrament belong together and need one another because Word and Sacrament confirm and explain one another. The Sacrament is the signature or sign which shows that the message is authentic, a true pointer to the mystery. The Word invites us to the table and promises that there we will meet the Lord who gave and gives himself to us. That's why Robert Bruce said so long ago in his wonderful sermons on *The Mystery of the Lord's Supper*:

> Thou obtainest a greater and surer holde of that same thing in the Sacrament than thou hadst by the hearing of the Worde. Then wilt thou aske what new thing we get? I say, we get this new thing: we get Christ better than before ... we gette a greater holde of Christ now.

It is he who invites us to his table to get a firmer grasp of him and of the mystery hidden from the learned and revealed here to the simple. This is what God did.

The Meal as Memory

Each of us carries a sack of memories around with us. Early in our lives, we start to stow away memories in our sack – memories of holidays, of school, of family, memories of sadness, memories of the high points and the low points of our lives. We remember tastes and smells and feelings.

A sack of memories is important for each one of us, for it tells us who we are, where we belong, our place in time and space. If we lose our sack of memories, or it is stolen from us, we are indeed in a predicament. A people that has been deprived of its history is a people that has lost its identity and is ready for enslavement or absorption by another people. A person who loses his or her memory, who has amnesia or dementia, doesn't recognise home or loved ones. To lose one's memory of the past is a kind of death.

Sometimes, our sacks become so heavy that we can hardly move. We wallow in memories. Our sacks weigh us down, burden us, packed tight as they are with memories we want to keep tied up and forgotten – painful memories, shameful memories, bitter memories, memories of broken relationships, memories of disagreements that cannot be resolved, sore and angry memories that we fear to let out. This is especially true for those whose early memories include pain, betrayal, rejection, humiliation or cruelty. How can they move on in their journey with this weight of memory? These are memories that need healing, reconciliation, forgiveness. And these memories will be revisited for fresh healing and love as the years go by.

Jesus, like most Jews, knew all about the taste of memory. At the great Passover feast,[7] celebrated annually down the ages, the family and the guests sitting around the table eat specific foods. It has changed somewhat over the ages and in different cultures and countries, but basically it is the same.

- They eat unleavened bread, *matzoth*, similar to water biscuit; this was the 'bread of affliction' that slaves ate, but especially they eat it because the Jews in Egypt had to escape before the dough had time to rise. It was 'fast food'.
- They eat bitter herbs to remind them of the bitterness of slavery in Egypt.
- They eat lamb shank to represent the sacrificial lamb in the temple and because the blood of a lamb on the lintels of their doors saved them from destruction.
- They eat a paste-like mixture of fruits and nuts, *haroseth,* cooked long and slow, which recalls the

mortar used by the Jewish slaves as they built for their masters – although some say it represents the mud through which they had to wade in order to escape.

- Then there is horseradish, the strongest kind, which draws tears from eyes, to remind them of their tears of affliction.

- There is a scorched hard-boiled egg, representing new birth through suffering – although some say the scorch-mark is to remind them of the destruction of the temple.

- Finally, they eat green fresh herbs, usually parsley, to celebrate the refreshing cycle of new life. But even the leaves are dipped in salt water to remind them of the tears of the past.

- In some countries, they eat a beetroot soup which suggests the Red Sea, through which they were delivered to freedom.

They taste the story of their past, which tells them who they are today. Then they proceed to re-enact, to retell the story, to sing the ancient Passover psalms, to possess the past afresh, to hand it on to a new generation, but above all, perhaps, to *taste* it. The past and the present are telescoped together. We are with Moses and Aaron and the people of Israel as they prepare for a hasty departure, as they are pursued across the Red Sea by Pharaoh's army, as they journey through the desert to the Promised Land. That story defines who we are. We receive the deliverance of God's people. The past comes alive for us. We taste and see that the Lord is good. Blessed are those who put their trust in him.

The New Passover[8]

And so it is with us. At the table of the Lord, we bring our sacks of memory. We can tell God of our memories of sadness and bitterness, regrets or failure. We come in this moment, this time in our lives, this particular day, and we re-enact and repossess the memory of what God has done for us in Christ. That story becomes our story. Here, we know ourselves to be free people, forgiven, released from the bondage of the past, delivered by God for his joyful service. When we take the bread and take the cup, the past becomes present; the Lord is with us, giving himself for us and to us. Here, we taste and see how good the Lord is. This meal tells us who we are. It joins us with the saints of every age and every land. It draws the past, the present and the future together. It nourishes us for our journey.

But the Lord's Supper is not a nostalgic, wistful longing for the past, or a wallowing in memories. It's not a solemn wake for a dead Jesus. Here, the past comes alive today. That's why we *celebrate* the presence of Jesus at the table. Jesus is alive – and here, at his table, he gives himself to us afresh. The Lord is risen! Here, he offers us bread and wine, food for our pilgrimage. Here, he is the host and giver of the feast. At this table, he welcomes each one of us to sit with him in companionship and love.

Questions for Discussion

1. Can we revive the sense that the Lord's Supper is a meal?

2. What kind of ethical commitment does participation in the Lord's Supper involve?

3. What are the implications of the table-fellowship of Jesus for our worship and our life?

Notes

1. Matthew 11:16–19 (NRSV).
2. Matthew 26:56 (NRSV).
3. John 21:1–14 (NRSV).
4. Luke 24:13–18, 28–35.
5. Luke 24:35 (NRSV).
6. Acts 2:42 (NRSV).
7. Deuteronomy 16:1–8.
8. Luke 22:7–20.

8

The Feast of the Future[1]

We have been considering how, in the Lord's Supper, memories come alive for us, the past and the present are telescoped together; we possess the past afresh, and above all *taste* it. But it is not just the past with which we should be concerned. We should also consider the Lord's Supper as a foretaste of the good things God has in store for us, an anticipation, the promise made real. It is an appetiser for the heavenly banquet that God has promised.

The meal in the upper room, the betrayal, the trial and the death of Jesus in pain and desolation all took place at Passover. For the authorities in Church and state, there was little that was strange about this. The temple guard and the Roman legions were on red alert. At Passover, one had to expect trouble. It had happened before and would happen again. At Passover, people were reminded that they were in God's eyes free people, that they were of infinite value to God, that God's purpose was to liberate them and save them. For the Jews, Passover was a time of expectation and of hope. For the Romans, it was a time of tension and uncertainty. Every Passover was a kind of protest against oppression and injustice and all that degrades human beings. At Passover time, there were often outbursts against the army of occupation, against the oppressors, against the exploiters. And the military stood by to put it down.

For them, the Jesus movement was just another dangerous protest which had to be suppressed ruthlessly. They condemned Jesus as a revolutionary, the leader of another Passover revolt, and they wrote on his cross: 'This is the King of the Jews'. The Romans and the priests were right. Jesus' Passover was a threat to the existing order of things. But it was a different sort of challenge from the protest movements that they had put down before and would suppress again and again. His Passover, which we celebrate every time we gather at his table, was and is a time of expectation, and of hope, and of protest. For here, in the fragment of bread and the sip of wine, we taste the future.

Ages ago, I was shopping in the local supermarket, at the cheese counter. 'Have you tried Bleu d'Auvergne?' the assistant asked. 'No', I said, suspiciously. 'Here, taste this bit', she said, cutting and giving me a fragment. To my surprise, it was delicious. And so, of course, I bought a slice, and the whole family delighted in it. That tasting in the supermarket was a succulent foretaste of good things to come.

Before a banquet or a celebration, we usually have an appetiser – a drink, some nibbles, not a lot, but it whets the appetite, it makes us hungry and eager for the good things to come: 'a banquet of rich fare for all the peoples, a banquet of wines well matured and richest fare, well-matured wines strained clear'.[2]

The Lord's Supper is like that: it whets the appetite, it makes us eager for the good things to come, it makes us long for the great banquet of God's kingdom.

But, of course, there's far more than our taste-buds involved. In the Lord's Supper, we experience just a little of what the kingdom of heaven is like.[3] What we find here makes us long for the future joy, fulfilment, fellowship and acceptance of the kingdom. Here, we find the flavour of the kingdom, the taste of the kingdom, the kind of relationships that belong to the kingdom. And this authentic, if fragmentary, experience of God's kingdom makes us eager, hungry, hopeful for the future fullness of that kingdom, and uneasy with much in the world around us, and in ourselves, and in our own relationships.

Think of the young man in the story Jesus told of the prodigal son. Like so many young people of today, he left home for a strange mixture of reasons. He quickly wasted all his cash. He was quite likely infected – today, it might easily have been with AIDS. He no doubt had experimented with alcohol and drugs, and sex. Gaunt, filthy, hungry, smelly, he turns to go home as a last resort. How can he ever fit in again? Surely he's forfeited his place in the family? He will need to work hard to regain his right to be treated as a member of the family. He plans his speech as he trudges home, a speech of apology and abasement. As he tramps homewards, his father sees him from far away and runs to meet and embrace him, filthy as he is. The finest robe is brought for him. A ring is put on his finger. The most joyful feast in the family's memory is organised: 'For this son of mine was dead and has come back to life; he was lost, and now is found.' That's the kind of feast we taste a little at the Lord's table, and will enjoy in its fullness in the future, when we too go home.

Consider what the Lord's table has meant to generations of Black Americans. Black people, who had been humiliated and oppressed by the structures of white society six days of the week, gather together each Sunday to experience a new definition of their humanity. At the Lord's table, the janitor, the road-sweeper, the single mother, the seamstress from the sweatshops become brothers and sisters.

> Every person becomes somebody, and one can see the people's recognition of their new-found identity by the way they walk, and talk, and 'carry themselves'. They walk with a rhythm of assurance that they know where they are going, and they talk as if they know the truth about which they speak.[4]

They have found at the table dignity, purpose and hope, that nothing in life can shake or deny. And so do we.

Decades later, a young black man, Barack Obama, before he became President of the United States, had the same experience on visits to Black churches in Chicago. He describes services where he heard the clarion call of hope. Week by week, the stories of the Old Testament, stories of courage in the face of adversity, audacity in the face of injustice and the triumph of right over wrong, encouraged congregations to believe that the same God was active in them. The God who stood with Moses and Aaron against insolent might also stood with them. If David could, in the strength of God, overcome Goliath, so may the weak and defenceless in Chicago today. The people possessed the stories. They walked in the stories.

They became Moses and David, Deborah and Hannah. The tears of the dispossessed were their tears. The triumphs of God's people became their triumphs. These stories enabled the Black congregations of Chicago to look back on their own history of slavery and injustice and weeping, not with shame but with hope. In hearing the Word preached, and in receiving the sacrament of communion, hope was born, the hope of the Christian community in the face of adversity. A new vision of justice and truth and freedom took root in their hearts and minds. People dared to believe in change.

The story is told of a survivor of Auschwitz. She was asked, forty years later, why she had survived when so many had perished. She told how, on arrival at the camp, she had been forcibly separated from her family, whom she never saw again, She had been stripped, her head had been shaved, and she had been herded into a shower with scores of other women. She had been given a shapeless, sack-like striped garment to put on, and driven into a huge shed where she had met a group of women who had been treated in the same way. Despair and terror had overwhelmed her. After a few moments, a young girl came over from the group, smiled, and thrust a small piece of bread into her hand. Years later, she was able to pinpoint that moment as the time she had decided to live. The bread had given her hope. It, like the bread and wine at the Lord's table, was the taste of the future.

The Lord's Supper is the feast of the future. Here, we are given hope as we taste a morsel of the future that God has in store for us. This is the appetiser for the heavenly banquet, which makes us hungry for the things of God. Here, we 'proclaim the Lord's death until he comes', when we too will sit at table with him.[5]

This is the Supper of the New Age, the meal of heaven, our tearful/joyful celebration today of God's tomorrow. We accept God's invitation to the feast and acclaim the coming victory of Christ. If we really believe that it is the Lord who invites us to sup with him, we should be really suspicious of churches that 'fence the table' or rigorously limit the invitation to the Lord's table. But this is by no means a rejection of the need for self-examination and confession as we prepare to approach the Lord's table.[6]

Intercommunion

Years ago, at a major ecumenical conference, I heard a leading Orthodox theologian give a magnificent paper in which he argued that, in the Eucharist, all human conflicts and hostilities are overcome, so that the Eucharist was the exemplar and reality of reconciliation. 'All human alienation and exclusiveness are eliminated in the Eucharist', he said. 'A new, Catholic humanity is created – a new family of human kind.' There was an enthusiastic and positive discussion. At the end of the session, another Orthodox priest got up and announced that, the following morning, there would be a celebration of the Holy Mysteries according to the Orthodox rite. And only the Orthodox would be allowed to receive communion. The priest seemed oblivious to the irony in his statement, how effectively it repudiated the argument in the magnificent paper we had just discussed. For me, it brought back memories of many Student Christian Movement conferences at which, on the Saturday evening, a leading Anglican would announce that he was deeply distressed that, at the communion the next day, only Anglicans would be allowed to receive the consecrated bread and wine. The irony of such situations was only too obvious, and it is good that some progress has been made in this area. Such relations among Christians have caused scandal – and sometimes amusement – among outsiders, who see clearly that there is a contradiction between what Christians say and how they behave in these matters.

The Shape of the Lord's Supper

There appear to be immense differences between the churches and the various Christian traditions in the name given to the central rite of Christian worship – the Mass, the Eucharist, the Lord's Supper, the Holy Mysteries, the Breaking of the Bread and so forth. The central symbols also appear to differ, as do the words and actions used. These differences are not trivial or unimportant, but, beneath them, there is a substantial unity which reminds us that they flow from the same source. This is the account of the origins of the Supper given to us by St Paul, which is used most commonly in Eucharistic services, either as part of the Great Thanksgiving or as a mandate read in the early part of the service. After dealing with the scandal of some wealthy believers stuffing themselves while others go hungry, and with divisions in the congregation, Paul declares that, in such a situation, it is not the Lord's Supper that is eaten – even, presumably, if the 'correct' words and actions are used by the correct people.[7] Paul continues:

> For I received from the Lord what I also delivered to you, that the Lord Jesus on the night when he was betrayed took bread, and when he had given thanks, he broke it, and said, 'This is my body which is for you. Do this in remembrance of me.' In the same way also the cup, after supper, saying, 'This cup is the new covenant in my blood. Do this, as often as you drink it, in remembrance of me.' For as often as you eat this bread and drink the cup, you proclaim the Lord's death until he comes.[8]

This passage reminds us that, despite all the great and sometimes contentious differences in the way Christians regard and celebrate the Lord's Supper, there is a common core of meaning and significance, which in modern times has in a sense been rediscovered by the Liturgical Movement and the services of worship that it has influenced.

The Last Supper that Jesus had with his disciples was either a Passover meal (according to the synoptic gospels) or shortly before the Passover, according to John, who emphasises that the death of Jesus, the true Passover Lamb, took place at the time when the Passover lambs were being sacrificed. Passover imagery shaped the Last Supper and provided an interpretation of the cross and resurrection. The movement from the Last Supper to the cross, and then the resurrection, was, and is, the heart of Christian faith and worship, and is freshly celebrated every time the Supper is observed: 'For our paschal lamb, Christ, has been sacrificed. Therefore, let us celebrate the festival . . .'[9]

At the Passover, the bread that is used is unleavened *matzoth*. This is why most Western churches use unleavened wafers in their Eucharistic services – medicinal to look at, tasteless in the mouth, and sometimes stamped with an image of Jesus on the cross to emphasise the radical difference between this and all other ordinary meals. It would be good to recapture and revive the sense that the Eucharist is indeed a meal, to be enjoyed, and charged with rich symbolism.

On a very hot summer's day, a group in my own congregation gathered around the Lord's table for communion. There was a woman there with Down's Syndrome. Her sister passed the cup to her with the words: 'Jesus loves you, Grace.' Grace took a generous mouthful, slaking her thirst, then wiped her mouth and said with satisfaction: 'That wis awfie guid' (That was awfully good). It would be good if the churches could recover a greater sense of the Eucharist as a meal to be enjoyed.

In the Reformed tradition, there was for long a great emphasis on the Lord's Supper as a meal. Communicants sat around long tables that were covered with linen cloths. The elements of bread and wine were passed from hand to hand to emphasise that each of us serves and is served by our neighbours.

The Ministry of the Word

All celebrations of the Lord's Supper divide into two parts – the Word and the Sacrament. These two parts belong together. The ministry of the Word is devoted to readings from the Bible, meditations, prayers, and discussion and preaching, all the time asking what God is calling us to be and to do today, facing the challenges and opportunities of the time. The prayers and hymns in this part of the service are mainly invocation, confession and intercession – prayers for the Church and the world, and for each other, that we may be faithful, holding up before God the challenges, and the suffering and the uncertainties of the day, and asking God's blessing. Three lessons are set in a lectionary – from the Old Testament, from the Epistles, and from the gospels. The sermon or homily explores the Biblical passages set for the day, and the challenges and opportunities for Christians and the Church.

The immediate response to the ministry of the Word is normally the Creed and the prayers of intercession, holding up before God the needs and activities and commitments of the congregation and the broader community in that particular time and place.

The Eucharist, the Supper, or the Mass has a movement, a pattern that is usually followed.

1. The **Offertory**, when representatives of the congregation bring forward to present to God the offerings of the people, together with the bread and the wine to be blessed and used in the service. The minister, who presides at the service, takes the offerings and blesses them.

2. The **Peace**, when greetings are exchanged with neighbours, has been restored to most liturgies in fairly recent times. It is not just a friendly gesture;

it is a powerful symbol of our love and care for our neighbours far and near, and our commitment to peace in the world, in the Church and in the local community.

3. The **Prayer**. A number of elements are usually included in the Eucharistic Prayer of Thanksgiving, in the past in Scotland often called the Action Prayer, perhaps as a reminder that the service should lead directly to loving action in the world. But, more likely, it is so called because the highest and the best, the purest and the most powerful cannot be spoken, but must be done or acted.

4. The **Sanctus** – Holy, holy, holy Lord – is a reminder that our worship is caught up with the worship of heaven, and that we are in fellowship with all the saints. It comes from Isaiah's vision of heaven 'in the year that King Uzziah died'.[10]

5. The **Anamnesis**, or memorial, is far more than a remembering of things long past. It is a constant renewed awareness of what God has done and is doing for us in Christ, and of his goodness to us day by day.

6. The **Epiclesis** invokes the Spirit to bring us into the presence of God, and awakens us to the presence of God among us and with us. The whole prayer finishes with a triumphant doxology, and with the Lord's Prayer.

7. The **Fraction** comes after the Action Prayer: the Fraction, the breaking of the bread, for the life of the world.

8. The **Sharing** of the bread and the wine, the communion, the fellowship of eating and drinking follows.
9. Last comes the **Blessing and Dismissal**, to go out and serve Christ in the life of the world, with all its agonies, injustices and conflicts, and its joys as well.

As Dom Gregory Dix reminds us in his magisterial *The Shape of the Liturgy*, the command of the Lord to celebrate the supper has been obeyed throughout the world and down the centuries. From birth to death, in sickness and in health, in joy and in grief, people have celebrated this supper. Families, communities, nations have re-enacted this supper for tragedy and for victory. In refugee camp or in palace, in country kirk or great cathedral, in prison chapel or at sea, this meal is celebrated. Above all, it is celebrated every Lord's Day in every country of the world. Young or old, confident or despairing, we hear the words 'This is my body given for you. This is the blood of the new covenant shed for the forgiveness of sins.' Therefore we bow our heads in gratitude and receive – one great community in earth and in heaven.

Questions for Discussion

1. How often should the Lord's Supper be celebrated?
2. 'Christ, our Passover is sacrificed for us. Therefore let us keep the feast.' Do you see a continuity between the Passover and the death of Jesus?

Notes

1. Isaiah 25:6-9.
2. Isaiah 25:6 (NEB).
3. Luke 15:11–32.
4. J. H. Cone, cited in Forrester et al., *Encounter with God*, 2nd edn (T&T Clark, 1996), p. 198.
5. 1 Corinthians 11:26 (NRSV).
6. 1 Corinthians 11:27–32.
7. 1 Corinthians 11:17–22.
8. 1 Corinthians 11:23–6.
9. 1 Corinthians 5:7–8 (NRSV).
10. Isaiah 6:1–3.

Conversing with God

Words and Silence

No words are adequate for our meeting with God which is at the heart of Christian worship. And yet Christian worship can be, and often is, full to overflowing with words. Words used by the leader may be copied from commentaries or, increasingly, downloaded from the Internet and may even be spoken without understanding! Above all, there is little time for silence or for unspoken prayer or for listening.

The story is told, which I hope may be true, of a gathering of leading Buddhists and prominent Christian leaders in Sri Lanka, intended to deepen their understanding of each other's faith. The Christians thought it would be good to start their session with a reading from the 'most spiritual' of the gospels, the Gospel according to John. 'In the beginning was the Word . . .', the leading Christian read. At this, the senior Buddhist present sighed deeply and exclaimed: 'Even in the beginning, was there no silence in your religion?' The question was well put. Silence is important. Lovers are often silent together. Sometimes, the deepest communication takes place in silence. But often, in fact, we are afraid of silence, and we all need to learn how to wait upon God in silence – a reality that the Quakers have sustained through their history, for Quaker meetings are largely silent to this day.

We must learn how to use silence, both in our own lives and in the worship of the Church. Perhaps we could use a prayer like this:

> We are so busy, Lord, we do not listen.
> The world is so noisy, Lord, we do not hear.
> We do not hear what the Spirit is saying to each one of us.
> We have been afraid of silence.
> Lord, teach us to use your gift of silence.
> Teach us, Lord.   Amen.

Prayer as Dialogue

Prayer is like a dialogue between God and us – a kind of conversation which sustains and depends on a relationship and is indeed virtually indispensable to that relationship. The relationship is continuous. Prayer in the sense of time set aside for this particular dialogue is not continuous, although prayerfulness, a prayerful attitude, should inform the whole of life.

In suggesting that prayer is to be understood on the analogy of dialogue or conversation – an image which must not be pushed too far – we are explicitly excluding the idea of prayer as magic or as a kind of shopping list. Magic is concerned with the control and manipulation of supernatural forces. A shopping list is a catalogue of demands. Neither is about relationship. Social use of language (in prayer or otherwise) is concerned with the establishing and nurture of relationships, with 'bonding', with the building of fellowship through communication. It also follows from this that Christians do not understand prayer primarily as self-exploration. It is, rather, an encounter with God which leads to self-examination and a deepening of self-understanding. Similarly, prayer should not be understood simply as a form of psychological hygiene, although prayer may well be cathartic or result in an improved sense of well-being and peace.

As we have seen, Jesus shocked the people of his time by teaching that we should approach God confidently, joyfully, simply as children coming to a loving parent. The use of the term *Abba* was so striking that it survives in its Aramaic form in the New Testament[1] and lies behind the slightly more formal 'Our Father' with which the Lord's Prayer begins. Like so much taught by Jesus, it is simple to say, and all but impossible to live.

It is important to recognise here that all human parenting is flawed. Most of us do our best; but even then, 'adequate' rather than 'perfect' is the adjective that comes to mind. Indeed, we know only too well that human fathers may be violent, abusive, ungenerous and, in some cases, altogether absent. For the children of such fathers, it may be very difficult ever to pray using the words which Jesus used. With penitence for all our fallen race, we, who lead worship, must be willing to explore the use of language to facilitate the closeness and generosity and depth of God's love for us. The word *Abba* is not *primarily* about relationship, it is about *intimacy*.

The Church down the ages has spent much energy trying to escape from the simplicity and directness of Jesus' teaching on prayer. His 'model prayer', the Lord's Prayer,[2] his own practice of prayer and the things he taught all suggest the availability of God to listen to prayer, a readiness to respond, and the similarity of prayer to conversation within a loving relationship. It is this basic conviction about the nature of God's approachability and loving responsiveness which gives Christian prayer its distinctive shape and mood and content.

The Place of Formulae

In everyday language we constantly use formulae – forms of words which lack precision or clarity, because it is the social function of the formulae which is important. We say 'hello' or 'hi', 'goodbye' or 'cheerio' simply as formulae of greeting or farewell. We send letters with 'yours sincerely' or 'yours faithfully', and it certainly does not guarantee the honesty or integrity of the writer. 'How do you do?' seems well on the way to ceasing to be a question expecting any answer. And, in Britain at least, many conversations start with a highly formulaic little exchange of comments about the weather.

Such formulae are a necessary part of social interaction. We teach our children to say 'please' and 'thank you' even when the words bear little relation to what the children are, in fact, feeling. These are not only signs of good manners but also tutors of feeling and a not unimportant part of the socialising process, the induction into a particular community and set of relationships. Much conversation never gets beyond the level of formulae – polite, cocktailparty chit-chat, often labelled 'small talk'. Indeed, formulae may be used as a way of avoiding real conversation, real dialogue, real encounter. We may even convert them into magical spells, or allow over-familiarity to deprive them of meaning. But there is also a sense in which formulae may be the preliminary to real conversation, the prelude to frank and fresh interaction. We can use formulae as a way of defending ourselves against real meeting, or as a kind of testing the water before we plunge into significant conversation.

Prayer, and particularly public prayer, is full of such formulae and set forms. Most of them are familiar and much loved, with all sorts of associations gathered around them. But, if you asked the members of an average congregation what 'Kyrie eleison', 'Amen' and 'Halleluia' mean, you would get a bewildering diversity of replies and, if people were honest, a large proportion of 'don't knows'. It would be interesting to know what worshippers today make of the phrase 'world without end' with which so many prayers are concluded. It is in fact an inaccurate translation of the Latin *in saecula saeculorum*, meaning 'for ever and ever' or 'throughout all ages'. The old phrase continues in use although it conveys either no meaning at all, or a misleading one.

Much of the language of public prayer is constantly repeated. This is as characteristic of most extempore prayer as it is of more formal liturgical prayer. Phrases, sentences and whole prayers such as the Magnificat, Nunc Dimittis and the Lord's Prayer are used so frequently in worship that reformers of a puritan inclination dismiss them as 'vain repetitions'. It is, however, a mistake based on a wrong translation of Matthew 6:7 to suggest that Jesus rejected the repetition of familiar forms in prayer. The Greek term *battalogein*, translated in the Authorised Version as 'use in vain repetitions', is better rendered as 'to heap up empty phrases' (RSV) or 'to go babbling on' (NEB). The clear intent of the verse as a whole is to discourage pointless verbosity in prayer rather than repetition. It would appear that Jesus himself used repetition in prayer,[3] as any pious Jew would be accustomed to doing, and did not see the new intimacy in prayer, into which he introduced his disciples, as excluding the use of set forms or in any way incompatible with participation in the formal prayers of the temple and the synagogue.

Like the formulae of everyday conversation, prayer formulae can be the preliminary to, and a training for, a more profound, spontaneous and direct dialogue.

My wife Margaret, raised in the Church of Scotland, with roots in the Free Church of Scotland, tells of how, as a student, she first heard the words of the General Thanksgiving. The scornful first reaction was 'vain repetition'. Then, as the language rolled over her, she listened with amazement and delight.

> Almighty God, Father of all mercies, we thine unworthy servants do give thee most humble and hearty thanks ... We bless thee for our creation, preservation, and all the blessings of this life; but above all for thine inestimable love in the redemption of the world by our Lord Jesus Christ, for the means of grace and for the hope of glory. (*Book of Common Prayer*, 1662)

The words rang around her ears like music and entranced her mind. Why had this treasury not been opened before? Although the General Thanksgiving is a very general and formal prayer, it has inspirational and sustaining depth.

The movement from the formal prayer to more authentic and revealing communication is often a penetration into the depths of meaning and imagery contained in the formulae. Thus the classic prayer, even as a formula, remains as guide, treasure, inspiration and comfort.

The Shape of Prayer

All prayer has a shape, a flow, a movement, a structure. Otherwise, it would be nothing but meaningless jumbles of words, phrases and sounds, very much the 'babbling on' that Jesus warned his disciples against in their prayers. All public prayer must have shape; but some prayers in shape and sequence are more spiritually and aesthetically satisfactory than others.

The various kinds of prayer may be classified either in terms of their purpose and content, or in terms of their structure and form. Not all are indispensable in every act of worship, but an awareness of the various types of prayer helps us to maintain a proper balance in worship. There is also a sequence, a development from one kind of prayer to another, which has been found in the experience of the Church to be psychologically and spiritually helpful, and to fit naturally into the movement of Christian worship. The various forms are not wholly distinct from one another and tend to flow together. Perhaps we should regard them as stepping stones, leading us onwards, individual yet connected.

Prayers may be classified in terms of their purpose and content. A list of the main types of prayer follows. This is roughly the order in which the prayers would come in a service of the Lord's Supper. It is important to recognise that prayer and the singing of psalms and hymns may be interchangeable. Thus, a great hymn of adoration may take the place of a prayer of adoration.

(a) *Adoration*. Here, at the start of worship, the worshippers remind themselves of the presence of God and turn their attention towards God with enjoyment, giving to God due glory and love. It thus sets the tone for the whole of worship: the focus is on God and not on ourselves, on God's wonderful love and power and faithfulness, rather than on our own feelings.

(b) *Invocation*. This is a prayer asking for God's presence and help in our worship, so that it may be worship 'in Spirit and in truth', acceptable to God and enlightening to his people.

(c) *Penitence or Confession*. Briefly, and early in the service, we think of ourselves in the light of the glory of God. This is not all about sin, at least not in a narrow individualistic sense. Some people come with burdens; some come with bitterness; some come with lost visions and ideals, with a dream that has died; and some come with a very specific wrongdoing or sin to confess. Shame, penitence and sorrow are expressed for all the ways in which we have fallen short of God's glory. In our brokenness, we seek God's forgiveness to restore the relationship – a forgiveness which is declared at the end of the prayer.

(*d*) *Supplication*. Still focusing on ourselves, and before we turn back to God and the needs of the world, the prayers of penitence and confession are naturally followed by a prayer for some special graces and for God's help in living as disciples.

(*e*) *Illumination*. In the context of the ministry of the Word, and usually before the sermon, or sometimes before the scripture readings, there comes a prayer that our minds may be illuminated so that we can hear and understand what God is saying to us and can respond with alacrity and joy. Again, this may well be in the form of a hymn – for example, 'Lord, thy word abideth' or 'Look upon us blessed Lord ...'.

(*f*) *Intercession*. At the beginning of the response to the Word of God, in the prayers of intercession, the needs of the Church and the world are offered to God, often in very specific terms, with people in need being prayed for by name and the issues of the day and the concerns of the congregation being remembered in some orderly sequence. The leader should use great sensitivity and discernment in praying for specific issues and remembering the reality of the world situation.

(*g*) *Thanksgiving for the Blessed Departed*. In churches of the Roman Catholic and Orthodox traditions, it is customary to pray for the dead and to ask the saints and the Virgin Mary to pray for us. The Reformation rejected prayers for the dead as superstitious and too closely tied to the belief in purgatory, and prayers for the intercession of the saints as impugning the sole mediatorship of Christ. Most Protestant churches now encourage a prayer which is a kind of extension of the prayer of thanksgiving (and may come at the end of that prayer rather than after the intercessions), giving thanks for the life of all the faithful departed, and asking that we may be strengthened to follow their example. It is desirable, however, that even those who feel continuing theological difficulties involved in prayers for the dead should be reminded that their prayers are joined with the prayers of all the saints in earth and heaven; and, in that sense, we pray with the saints in heaven and they presumably pray for us, even if we feel it inappropriate to pray for them!

(h) *Thanksgiving*. This is at the heart of the Great Prayer of the Lord's Supper. In a real sense, thanksgiving, the praise and glorification of God, is the heartbeat at the centre of all prayer. Thanksgiving is accordingly most properly one of the climaxes of a service, whether or not that service be a celebration of the Lord's Supper. It is placed at this point in the service because thanksgiving is the dominant note in the response to the declaration of God's truth and love in the ministry of the Word. We give thanks for what God has done and will do – leading naturally to a commitment to his service.

(i) *Oblation*. In this prayer, the whole Church, individual Christians in fellowship with one another, with the Body of Christ in every land and every age, and with the Risen Lord, offer themselves to the Father to be used for the work of the kingdom. In the Lord's Supper, this prayer commonly comes at the end of the Great Thanksgiving; in other services, it may appropriately be allied to the dedication of the offerings of the people.[4]

Prayers may also be classified in terms of their structure or form.

1. *Collect.* This highly developed and much-loved form of prayer has a simple and clear structure, encourages succinctness and is often of great beauty. Collects usually consist of six parts: (1) an address to God; (2) a relative clause indicating the activity or attribute of God on the basis of which we approach him; (3) the petition; (4) the purpose of the petition; (5) a doxology; and (6) the conclusion declaring the sole mediatorship of Christ. For example:

> Almighty God,
> to whom all hearts are open,
> all desires known,
> and from whom no secrets are hidden;
> cleanse the thoughts of our hearts
> by the inspiration of your Holy Spirit,
> that we may perfectly love you
> and worthily magnify your holy name;
> through Christ our Lord.
>
> (*Common Order*, First Order for
> Holy Communion, p. 122)

Some of the parts may be omitted, but a collect is always terse and follows strict rules of rhythm and development. Not all short prayers are collects; and the collect is only one of the forms of prayer available. Collects have a significant place in worship, particularly at the start of the worship (when people are collected), or as a summing-up of prayers or of the theme of the ministry of the Word. But public prayer should never be allowed to become great strings of collects and nothing else.

2. *General prayer*. This is a prayer whose content is general rather than specific. It is usually longer and more loosely constructed than a collect; but classic prayers of this sort such as the General Confession and General Thanksgiving of the *Book of Common Prayer*, the Prayer for the Whole Estate of Christ's Church in the Church of Scotland *Book of Common Order*, 1940 (itself derived from a similar prayer in the *Book of Common Order* of 1564) and indeed the Lord's Prayer itself are splendid instances of English prose – dignified, lucid and musical. The danger with general prayers is that they tend to become verbose and lacking in unity unless very skilfully composed. And, by definition, their content is general rather than specific to the time, place and congregation.

3. *Bidding prayer*. In this form of prayer, a list of subjects for prayers of thanksgiving or intercession is given out, sometimes using responses or followed by a period of silence and a brief prayer summing up the prayers offered. Most modern liturgies suggest this form for the prayers of intercession. It has the virtues of being highly adaptable and combining extempore elements – or even spontaneous prayer from members of the congregation – and set forms within a clear and simple structure.

4. *Litany*. This is a responsive prayer, rather like a bidding prayer, but usually excluding any extempore or spontaneous elements. Many of the older litanies, such as that in the English *Book of Common Prayer* or those in the *Scottish Book of Common Prayer* (1929), are comprehensive and lengthy prayers, really amounting to a special office in their own right. Modern litanies, such as the two litanies of intercession in the Church of South India *Book of Common Worship*, are far shorter and almost indistinguishable from bidding prayers. Many of the traditional litanies can still appropriately be used in whole or part on special occasions, but are too long and often too archaic to be used frequently.

5. *Acclamations*. Many modern liturgies have restored this ancient form of prayer said, sung or shouted out by the people. In the Eucharistic prayer of the Roman Mass and in the Anglican communion, the people say immediately after the words of institution:

> Christ has died,
> Christ is risen,
> Christ will come again

or another brief acclamation. Most other modern forms of worship also have acclamations for the people. In addition, the *Sanctus* and *Benedictus* are more properly classified as acclamations than as responses.

6. *Versicles* and *responses*. These are short responsive prayers, sometimes used as an introduction to a prayer, sometimes forming a shorter litany in an office such as the

Book of Common Prayer Matins, or the Office of Compline. Examples of these are:

> Versicle: Lord, in your mercy
> Response: Hear our prayer.

Or:

> Versicle: Lord, hear us
> Response: Lord, graciously hear us.

7. *Free Prayer.* For a long time, charismatic sects were the main groups that allowed members of the congregation to have a 'speaking role' in public prayer, apart from set responses and prayers said together. It has, however, become common in most of the mainstream denominations for opportunities to be given to members of the congregation to pray aloud, particularly in the prayers of intercession, confession and thanksgiving. The reintroduction of this primitive practice is often met with some initial but short-lived embarrassment, yet it is quickly accepted as a privilege which adds reality to prayer and greatly improves the sense of participation as well as blending surprisingly well with the more formal prayers.

The Movement of Prayer

All prayer has a shape, which may be more or less adequate. It was Calvin who reminded us that, if we use a correct form in transacting business, which is required by public and human decency, then this ought also to be observed in churches. This applies whether the prayers in question are an ancient or modern set form, composed for the occasion (or 'conceived' prayers, to use Isaac Watt's phrase), extempore (not prepared word for word before the service), or free, when members of the congregation may lead in prayer as they wish and the Spirit moves. The single most important reason why shape or form is important in public worship is that it is far easier for the members of the congregation to appropriate and make their own clear, well-structured prayer than to enter into a disjointed and loosely structured prayer. This may be perfectly appropriate in private or small-group prayers, but does not 'work well' in the necessarily rather more formal setting of public worship.

There is an emerging ecumenical consensus that there is a proper place in public worship for all these kinds of prayer, that they blend well together, and that this provides a more balanced experience of prayer for the congregation than the use of one kind alone. The great classical prayers, together with the best modern prayers, remind worshippers of the great heritage of Christian devotion, broaden and deepen their spiritual horizons, remind them that they pray in solidarity with the whole Church, and are so rich that they can be used again and again without exhausting their meaning. Extempore, composed or free prayer allows for the freedom of the Spirit and recognises that it is a particular congregation in a particular place at a particular time which is praying and has specific matters to bring before the Lord. A sensible combination of these kinds of prayer in public worship shows that they complement and fertilise one another, and together enrich and enliven the congregation's experience.

Questions for Discussion

1. 'Prayer is like a dialogue between people and God, a kind of conversation ...' Do you agree?
2. How may we avoid 'vain repetition' in prayer?

Notes

1. Mark 14:36; Galatians 4:6; Romans 8:15.
2. Matthew 6:9–13; Luke 11:2–4.
3. Matthew 26:44.
4. This list is somewhat indebted to that in Raymond Abba, *Principles of Christian Worship* (London, 1957), pp. 87–96. Cf. the *Book of Common Order of the Church of Scotland* (Edinburgh, 1994).

10

The Word beyond Words

True prayer is spontaneous, honest, personal and from the heart; it is a kind of lovers' discourse. And lovers' conversation is not always very polished or grammatical or coherent. What matters is that it comes from the heart, even when the heart is sad or confused or questioning.

Lovers often communicate in silence, gazing into one another's eyes, or sitting quietly side by side, holding hands and simply enjoying each other's company with a quiet confidence and joy. In worship, too, there is an important place for silence, the quiet in which the congregation together can enjoy the company of God. Most people need some training in the use of silence in prayer, and some preparation for it, otherwise the time of silence may have an atmosphere of tenseness, the uneasy quiet of those who expect every moment to be filled with words. The silence in prayer should be the silence of lovers, enjoying one another; the silence in which one appropriates and adds to the spoken prayers; and, above all, the silence in which the worshipper stops chattering and listens to the Word, to the other party in the dialogue of silence.

The Language of Prayer

Christian prayer is properly in the common tongue, in ordinary speech. In this, Christianity differs from many other religions which make an emphatic distinction between the sacred language used in worship, and often not understood by the people, and the profane language of everyday discourse. The tendency to use a special language for worship is widespread, and it is often felt that it is proper if the language of prayer is not understood. The obscurity and specialness of the language safeguards and emphasises the mystery. At the time of Jesus, a large number of Jews did not understand the Hebrew of the scriptures and the synagogue prayers. The scriptures were read, first in Hebrew, and then a *Targum*, or paraphrase in Aramaic, the *lingua franca* of the Levant, so that the people got the gist of what had been read in the unknown sacred tongue.

It would appear that, from the beginning, Christians believed that prayer should not be in a strange and sacred language; ordinary language was the appropriate vehicle for the new and intimate kind of communication between God and people which had been made possible by Jesus. Early Christian prayer may have been commonly in Aramaic – so the survival of words such as *Abba* and *Maranatha* in the New Testament would suggest. And, from early times, it is clear that Christians used the Septuagint, the Greek translation of the Jewish scriptures, in preference to the Hebrew. The earliest Christian documents to have survived, including many prayers, are in Greek – not classical educated Greek, but *koine* Greek, the crude and unpolished Greek of the marketplace, the language of most of the Mediterranean basin. Time and again in the early centuries of the Church, there is evidence to suggest that there were no doubts or hesitations about the need to translate the Bible and the liturgy into the language actually spoken by the people.

However, there appears to be an inherent tendency towards archaism and contrived mystery in the language of prayer; and gradually this infected the Christian Church. By the ninth century, some theologians were arguing that only the three languages of the superscription on the cross – Hebrew, Latin and Greek – were legitimate for Christian worship. These three were recognised as 'sacred tongues'; the emerging vernaculars were profane and undignified.

The most obvious example of the perpetuation in worship and church usage of an archaic language which only a small and declining minority understand is the use of Latin in the West. Originally adopted as the language of the people (rather than Greek, which had become the language only of the scholarly elite), Latin spread throughout the Western Church, eclipsing almost all vernacular forms of worship, eventually becoming for most worshippers a mysterious and unintelligible sacred tongue. This, of course, drastically affected the quality of participation possible for the laity worship. A strange tongue excluded the people from meaningful participation in worship, as this letter from Bishop Stephen Gardiner to Cranmer in 1547 makes clear:

> For in times past ... the people in the church took small
> heed what the priests and the clerks did in the chancel, but

only to stand up at the Gospel and kneel at the Sacring, or else every man was occupied himself severally in several prayer ... It was never meant that the people should indeed hear the Matins or hear the Mass, but be present there and pray themselves in silence.[1]

In 1661, Pope Alexander VII denounced those who had reached such a degree of madness that they had translated from the Roman Missal into French. He maintained that doing this both debased the majesty of the Latin language and exposed the sacred rites to the eyes of ordinary people.

As late as 1947, Pope Pius XII argued for the retention of Latin on the grounds of unity and as a safeguard against the corruption of true doctrine. But there are other, and better, ways in which worship may express the unity of the Church; and, even if the Latin liturgy expresses orthodox doctrine verbally, it certainly does not effectively communicate this doctrine, and it opens the way to all sorts of strange distortions and eccentric misunderstandings of the faith on the part of ordinary people. In addition, the use of a special 'church language' such as Latin emphasises the difference between clergy and laity – the elite who know and use the cultic language, and the majority who are mystified by it.

The Reformers, with rare unanimity, affirmed that the vernacular, the language of the people, should be the language of prayer, just as they stressed the central importance of putting the Bible, carefully translated, into the hands of the people. Luther was very clear that we must speak in church as we do at home, in our own language so that everyone can understand. In this, as in so much else, the Reformation strove to recover the emphases and practices of the early Church: the whole people of God should participate fully in worship, and this is impossible without understanding. The unnecessary and artificial mystery of an unknown tongue must be removed if the true mystery of faith is to become accessible. The use of a dead language in worship which few could understand was to be rejected. Understanding was the key. In the epistles, we read of Paul's ruling that speaking in ecstatic tongues should always be interpreted so that the people could understand. Cranmer was typical of the Reformers in believing that the move to vernacular in worship was clearly in accordance with the will of God.

The move to the 'plain mother tongue' did not, of course, mean that the languages of liturgy and of Bible translation became conversational or marketplace vernacular. The Reformers believed in the use of clear, simple and dignified language; and their most noticeable productions, such as the Anglican *Book of Common Prayer*, Luther's Bible, and the Authorised Version, did much to shape and encourage the development of the vernacular.

But the norms of liturgical English laid down between 1550 and 1662 tended to ossify while the 'plain mother tongue' developed vastly. This is as true of extempore prayer as of the authorised forms, for the language of the former was dominated by the Authorised Version and increasingly demonstrated the inbuilt conservatism of liturgical language. As a consequence, a good deal of the language of prayer has become opaque and obscure to many worshippers, and sometimes conveys a very different message from that originally intended. Not many worshippers today realise that

'Prevent us, O Lord' in the familiar collect means 'Go before us, O Lord, to enable us' rather than 'Stop us from doing'. The schoolboy who, when asked what 'divers temptations' might be, replied 'Might have been mermaids' was simply demonstrating an extreme case of the misunderstanding generated by the continued use of a cultic language which is now so different from the 'plain mother tongue' of everyday usage. Another complication is that some archaic English has acquired in the passage of time sexist overtones which are understood as excluding a goodly part of most congregations. Even some recent liturgies are replete with gratuitous sexism – 'fellow men' instead of 'we or us', 'all men' instead of 'everyone', and 'men' where 'people' is really meant.

The importance of not using exclusive language in worship can hardly be too strongly emphasised. A faith which has at its heart reconciliation and the overcoming of division and hostility should never in its worship use language which makes whole categories of people feel excluded from the community and from the loving purposes of God. It is not always easy or appropriate to modify or change exclusive language in older material; but modern worship language should be constantly sensitive to this issue.

Most churches now agree that, in worship, there must be explicit recognition of the feminine qualities of the Godhead. ('So God created humankind in his image, in the image of God he created them; male and female he created them': Genesis 1:27.) In worship and theology down the ages, there has been an unbalanced stress on the masculinity of God, whereas the Biblical imagery in both Old and New Testaments is much wider. It is worth noting here that the word for the Spirit in the Old Testament is *ruach*, and is female. In the New Testament, the word is *pneuma* and is neuter.

A rather different, but no less serious, problem arises from the continued use of the pronouns 'thee' and 'thou' in addressing God. In the sixteenth and seventeenth centuries, these were, in English as their equivalents are still in other European languages, the intimate terms used in family life or between close friends. 'You' was the more deferential form, used in addressing someone of great status and power. As late as the reign of Charles II, a Quaker woman caused a public outcry by addressing the king as 'thou' – it was considered an impertinence. The Reformers' choice of 'thou'-language in addressing God was indeed a daring affirmation of what one might call the '*Abba* principle', that our relationship with God is intimate and loving.

But, since the seventeenth century, 'thou'-language, with all its complicated impediments of verbal inflections, has fallen out of common usage. Except in prayer, no one addresses anyone else as 'thou'; and all the associated forms – thy and thine, wilt and shalt, didst and so forth – have so fallen into disuse that those who lead in prayer frequently land themselves in comic and unnecessary confusions. But the real problem is that the development of the English language and the entropy of liturgical English have led to an exact reversal of the original, theologically well-grounded reason for choosing to address God as 'thou'. Today, some people argue that this preserves a sense of the glory and the transcendent otherness of God, and discourages too easy a familiarity. But it was precisely intimacy and familiarity which Jesus offered in teaching us to come to God as *Abba*, and which the Reformers tried to safeguard by addressing God as 'thou'. Today, sound theology demands that 'thou', with all its quaint linguistic accompaniments, be set aside in Christian prayer.

It has to be admitted, however, that there is still a vast, intractable problem in finding an appropriate and satisfactory English style and idiom for public worship – always remembering that no language can possibly be adequate for speaking with God, or for speaking of God.

There are three important points here. First, the language of prayer does not come from nothing. The language of prayer is the language of a community, a community founded on the community's book, the Bible. Therefore, the language of the Bible provides a kind of map or reference guide where people who worship can locate the images and ideas, the references and the stories which are used in worship. It is still ordinary language, but language used in a special way.

The second thing to note is that, because prayer is not a self-contained language, it carries dangers of familiarity. Because prayer uses ordinary language, it can degenerate into trite phrases and banal literalism. Those who lead worship must use language sensitively and beautifully, penetrating to the depths and lifting to the heights to show the riches and the possibilities so often neglected in the modern world.

The third issue here is that the language of prayer is replete with images, metaphors, symbols and narrative – much, but not all of it, borrowed from scripture. Some of this material is vibrant and living. Other images, metaphors and symbols seem dormant, or dead and incapable of resuscitation. It would seem that one of the functions of liturgy is to preserve a treasury of images and symbols from which each generation finds some that are meaningful. Sometimes, an image that had seemed long dead is suddenly reborn and discovered to be relevant to a new situation – for example, the use of the word 'apocalypse' and associated vocabulary to understand and respond to global terrorism. Other symbols seem inaccessible and unrecoverable, embedded totally in ancient contexts alien to the modern experience. To find fresh imagery which can act as a vehicle for Christian prayer and communicate at the depth of the old is no easy task.

Some modern liturgical work uses fresh, contextual imagery and is both clear and has timeless dimensions. A flourishing of new hymn-writers in Scotland was started by Ian Fraser and John Bell. The latter's work in particular has encouraged people to sing new songs and to be creative in liturgy. The same is true in other parts of the world. In particular, *Together in Song*, Australian Hymn Book II, and *Uniting in Worship*, the worship book of the Uniting Church in Australia, both have contemporary integrity and classic beauty.

'What language shall I borrow, to praise thee, heavenly Friend?' No language, ancient or modern, is really adequate for prayer, for converse with God. As St Paul tells us,[2] when we use the finest of words, 'the tongues of mortals and of angels', without love, we become noisy gongs and clanging cymbals. The language of worship is the language of love, which is often simple and fragmentary but comes from the heart and speaks to the heart.

Questions for Discussion

1. What kind of language in prayer do we find most helpful?
2. In what way is prayer different from an inner dialogue in which one talks with oneself?
3. Is there a place for silence in prayer?

Notes

1. Cited in R. Abba, op. cit., pp. 23–4.
2. 1 Corinthians 13:1 (NRSV).